KILLER THINKING

Also by Tim Duggan

Cult Status: How to Build a Business People Adore

KILLER THINKING

How to Turn Good Ideas into Brilliant Ones

Tim Duggan

PANTERA
PRESS

PANTERA
PRESS

First published in 2022 by Pantera Press Pty Limited
www.PanteraPress.com

Please send all permission queries to:
Pantera Press, P.O. Box 1989, Neutral Bay, NSW, Australia 2089 or info@PanteraPress.com

A Cataloguing-in-Publication entry for this book is available from the National Library of Australia.

ISBN 978-0-6489874-6-8 (Paperback)
ISBN 978-0-6489876-0-4 (eBook)

Cover Design: Vanessa Ackland
Publisher: Lex Hirst
Project Editor: Tom Langshaw
Copyeditor: Kate O'Donnell
Proofreader: Cristina Briones
Typesetting: Kirby Jones
Internal Illustrations: Elysia Clapin
Author Photo: Cybele Malinowski
Printed and bound in Australia by McPherson's Printing Group

The paper this book is printed on is certified against the Forest Stewardship Council' Standards. McPherson's Printing Group holds FSC' chain of custody certification SA-COC-005379. FSC' promotes environmentally responsible, socially beneficial and economically viable management of the world's forests.

For Ben, who sat beside me as I wrote most of this travelling around Australia in our campervan.

Contents

KILLER THINKING

How to Turn Good Ideas into Brilliant Ones

Introduction

This is a book about ideas.

Those slippery, squishy, malleable thoughts that float into your head at the most unexpected times and then waft away just as quickly. If caught at the right time, and bent into the correct shape, ideas have the potential to transform industries, movements and lives.

Our world needs better ideas right now. Everywhere you look is an escalating problem – from the climate crisis to new ways of working to how to build better businesses to having more meaningful relationships – and creativity can help us tackle all these. Both the small problems that affect just a few people and the massive existential ones that threaten our very future need creative solutions.

Most people think of ideas as a renewable resource that will always be there whenever we need them. If we miss one, we tell ourselves, we'll just wait for the next idea to come along, as though they're peak-hour buses on a busy street. 'You can't use up creativity,' wrote American poet Maya Angelou. 'The more you use, the more you have.'

But I'll let you in on a little secret: ideas are plentiful, but they aren't all equal. In the same way that everyone can sing, there's a gaping difference between my off-key shower belting and Adele's expert control of her vocal ranges.

The good news is that, unlike my singing, creativity is a mindset everyone can master. You can learn how to separate some of the thought bubbles from the thousands that pop into your head, then refine and massage them until they have multiple positive outcomes for yourself and others.

Good ideas are everywhere you look. Most businesses are built on the back of a good idea. Richard Branson says, 'A business is simply an idea to make other people's lives better.' It might be selling a product or a service that solves a problem for someone, or an idea that improves your work or personal life. You can come up with a simple idea on your own without having to sit down and read an entire book about it.

Then there are **great ideas**, the ones that benefit more people beyond just making money for a few. Great ideas are less common, and are often refined versions of good ones that have had longer to evolve into something better that can have a bigger impact on more people. It takes some skill to turn a good idea into a great one, and they should be celebrated in every way. Most people with great ideas stop when they reach that level, happy to have elevated it above the others, but miss out on its full potential.

And then at the very top of the creativity ladder are **killer ideas**. The simplest definition of a killer idea is that an almost infinite number of people benefit from it. They are the kind of rare ideas that have an impact on many people in lots of ways, including the person who came up with the idea, the business and/or community it exists in, the environment, its customers, suppliers and more. Killer ideas have a lot of winners when they are successful, and very few drawbacks.

In this book you're going to learn how to come up with your own killer ideas, and the steps needed to move an idea along the conveyor belt from a good idea into a killer idea, and finally how to bring it to life. It might be an idea for how to be more efficient at work, a business idea, how to help people with a for-impact company, ways to make society fairer or more interesting, or just how to have some fun and make the world around you a little bit better.

I've always been drawn to killer ideas, the type you hear about and think, 'Damn! I wish I'd thought of that!' I've spent the better part of two decades playing with ideas and creativity as I built and sold the company I co-founded, Junkee Media, published my first book, *Cult Status*, and worked on lots of fulfilling long-term projects with companies like Netflix, American Express and Qantas. Alongside a graveyard of creative concepts that never went anywhere, I've brought to life a lot of good ideas, some great ones and, fortunately, a few that have stood the harsh test of time.

The first killer idea I accidentally created was an event series I started in my early twenties. Like most random thoughts that pop into our heads, it started out as just a decent, simple idea. I was bored with the usual venues for my fellow LGBT+ community to go out in my hometown of Sydney, so I sent an email to some friends asking them if they wanted to come with me to 'tag' a traditionally straight venue by all turning up at the same time on the same night (I jokingly called the event 'FagTag' without thinking too much about it). This easily understood idea spread quickly and a hundred or so attendees received a password that would get them a discount on the entry fee. It wasn't a revolutionary idea, but it worked.

If I had left the idea alone and not changed it at all, it probably would have died out naturally after a few events, but instead I kept refining the concept based on feedback, intuition and, let's face it, a little bit of my own boredom.

The initial idea was good, but people coming along to the events still had to pay to enter, and there were some unexpected tensions when large LGBT+ groups would turn up at a traditionally 'straight' venue without any notice. So I set about refining the idea. The first change was to completely take over an empty venue, rather than trying to mix with unaware crowds. The second change was to make it completely free, so it was accessible to more people. Those two small changes turned it from a good idea into a great one, and its popularity grew and grew until a few thousand people would turn up after I sent out a few emails to my database.

The final part of the equation was making it work for me so it was repeatable and could be long lasting. As the organiser of the event, I needed to be rewarded in some way or it wouldn't be sustainable to keep throwing it every month. I mapped out all the possible revenue models and settled on a simple one. As the events attracted lots of people who came to a venue and then spent money on food and drinks for themselves and their friends, I negotiated with each venue that I would get paid 10 per cent of the bar takings while the event was on. After experimenting with locations dotted all over the city, I also decided to return to some of the most iconic venues in the country, like the stunning Opera Bar. This is situated at the base of the Opera House and allows you to take a beer right down to the edge of Sydney Harbour and watch the world sail past. It really is one of the best bar locations in the world, and every summer for over 15 years, until Covid-19 got in the way, we returned to this venue.

It was there one late afternoon, as the orange rays of the setting sun reached through the arches of the Harbour Bridge, that I realised this was my first properly killer idea. It didn't start out that way, but I'd refined and evolved it over the years, keeping the same idea at its heart but constantly tweaking it until there were multiple winners. Lots of parties walked away with positive benefits including the thousands of patrons who turned up for free events, the live singers and DJs who got extra bookings, the venues and their staff who got extra shifts and tips, the LGBT+ community who felt stronger, community groups like ACON (a queer community-health organisation) who took advantage of large crowds to hand out educational flyers, and me – I received a healthy commission just for sending out a few emails to a database I'd built up over the years. I know of many friendships, marriages and even children born as a direct result of people meeting at these events. It was my first taste of what it takes to come up with a good idea, bring it to life and then keep tweaking it until it benefits lots of parties. Since then I've used the same principles to start multiple award-winning media titles like Same Same, Junkee, Punkee and AWOL, and keep pushing ideas along the spectrum from a good idea to a better one.

A good idea is a win for usually one or two parties, a great idea has several winners, but killer ideas are win times infinity as they have the potential to make the world around them better. Of course, nothing in this world is completely black and white, and every great idea has unintended consequences that occasionally creep in. But, for the whole part, the best ideas in the world have benefits that far outweigh their drawbacks.

To help you identify or come up with ideas that have big potential, I'm going to introduce you to a new framework through which you can run your creative output to ensure it is ticking all the boxes. In the past, a lot of killer ideas were the ones that made the most money, for their founders, shareholders and those lucky enough to be in the right place at the right time. We need to redefine what a killer idea is for our new century, and it's a fresh type of thinking that takes into account everyone around us. The very name of a killer idea is the best way of remembering what makes them stand out.

The best ideas in the world are KILLER:

Kind

Impactful

Loved

Lasting

Easy

Repeatable

We'll run through each of these in detail later in the book.

In writing and researching *Killer Thinking* I spoke with the creators of some of the best ideas in the world. You're about to meet the brains behind dozens of killer ideas and execution, like these ones:

- Turn discarded waste into useful household products
- Close down the streets of a city to cars one day a week
- Save shipping costs by dehydrating common products
- Prepare and cook fish in the exact same way as meat
- Democratise graphic design so anyone can do it
- Empower people experiencing homelessness to become micro-entrepreneurs
- Reuse the same takeaway coffee cup over and over

You might recognise a few of the businesses and movements above just from their summarised descriptions, but they all began as a momentary thought that flitted inside the head of someone who luckily had enough insight to recognise it as a good idea and the drive to work with it until the idea became a brilliant one.

In the past the positive impact of a killer idea might have been confined to one town or community, but today killer ideas are able to break out of where they begin and positively impact lots of people all at once.

The problems ahead of us are huge, and we require a new way of thinking to solve them. From coming up with ideas to avoiding pitfalls, creativity is a skill that's just as useful whether you have entrepreneurial dreams of running your own business or are an employee of a company. If you want to create the next impactful company or a social movement that'll change the world, the thinking behind these goals is the same.

In my first book, *Cult Status*, I wrote that there are two types of people in this world, and all of us fall neatly into one camp or the other:

> The first are the creative types. They're the ones who approach old ideas in new ways. They apply their creative thinking to their work, a hobby, a talent or their family. They have deep imaginations they're able to tap into to pull ideas seemingly out of nowhere. They might work for themselves, for someone else or start their own companies, and if they choose to focus their creativity on business they're able to concentrate their energy on building something with passionate customers who go wild for what they do. They are the first type of people in the world. The second type of people are dead. I genuinely believe that everyone has the ability to be creative in life and business: it's just that some people haven't had the chance to show us their skills yet. We're all creative in our own ways, with ideas percolating in the background – and we sometimes need help and external motivation to make those ideas concrete.

Little did I realise that short paragraph was going to worm its way into my head, only to shuffle out the other side a few years later as this book you're now reading.

Killer Thinking is for anyone who wants better ideas in their lives to help them solve problems. Some of these might be at work if you need to come up with a fresh, creative approach to help you grow your revenue or number of customers, or it may be a new way of thinking about something at home.

However, a book that's just about ideas is only half written; the next challenge is actually bringing it to life. An idea that's not realised is a waste of thought, and you've got to put just as much energy into the execution itself. That's why this book will cover killer ideas *and* killer execution. Combine the two of them and you've got killer thinking, and that's exactly what our world needs a lot more of right now.

The Key to Killer Thinking

Creativity is a wild, wonderful and messy process. If you study it closely enough, you can see some patterns emerging from all of the noise. While there is no foolproof formula to creativity, there is a series of steps you can perform that will bring you closer to coming up with and refining your own ideas until they are as good as they can be.

To help guide you through this, we're going to think of the steps to creating, refining and launching killer ideas in a visual way. This will help bring something concrete to some of the more theoretical ideas, and help keep track of where we are in the process. Every single person has potential killer thinking inside them – you just need confidence and knowledge to unlock them.

Throughout this book we're going to use the image of a keyhole, built one step at a time, to keep us on track and following our method in the right order. Each step will construct the keyhole from the bottom to the top, guiding you with examples and practical exercises, until you've created your own path to unlocking brilliant ideas you can use to turbocharge your work and personal life.

At the top of the next page is the key to Killer Thinking:

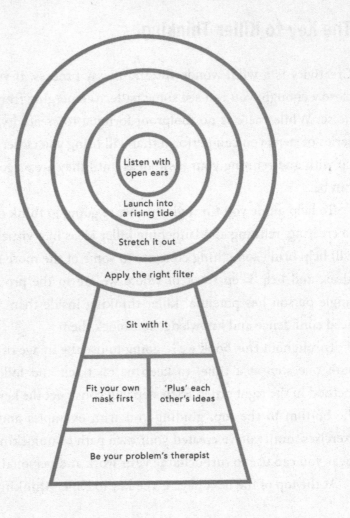

Listen with
open ears

Launch into
a rising tide

Stretch it out

Apply the right filter

Sit with it

Fit your own
mask first

'Plus' each
other's ideas

Be your problem's therapist

Six of the steps you're about to learn are devoted to the art of coming up with better ideas, and the last two to executing them expertly.

Step 1: Be Your Problem's Therapist

Before you dive into the fun part of coming up with creative solutions, you need to understand every single aspect of your problem better than anyone else. Take the time at the beginning of a project to absorb as much information as you can, and try looking at it from every angle.

Step 2: Fit Your Own Mask First

The biggest mistake most people make when trying to come up with ideas is to prematurely connect with others and try to do it together. Group creative sessions are useful, but they are a thousand times more effective when you do individual ideation first. You need to put on your own mask before you can properly help others fit theirs.

Step 3: 'Plus' Each Other's Ideas

This is the fun part, where you bring people together to come up with ideas collectively, using a simple method to build on top of others' ideas. I'll explain why most people are doing group creative sessions the wrong way, and how to compensate for that to generate dozens of fresh ideas with any group of people.

Step 4: Sit with It

You have to let ideas percolate into something special, and give them space, inputs and time to breathe. Without letting creativity work its magic, you're not going to get the most creative solutions to your problems.

Step 5: Apply the Right Filter

Once you've got some good ideas, you need a clear, fit-for-purpose filter that allows you to narrow down your idea to just the elements with the biggest potential. In this step you'll learn the best way to use predetermined criteria to sort through the ideas.

Step 6: Stretch It Out

Good ideas can be consciously stretched into great ones, and maybe even killer ones, if you concentrate on maximising the number of parties who will benefit. Use the simple technique of Winners and Losers to help massage ideas and move them along the scale.

Step 7: Launch into a Rising Tide

The timing of when you launch an idea is almost as important as the idea itself. In this step you'll meet lots of people who credit their fortuitous timings with some of their success, and understand global trends that will help guide the timing of your launch.

Step 8: Listen with Open Ears

Your idea is finally out in the world and people are using it and giving feedback. Knowing the difference between listening and hearing is the key to making your idea a killer one that has potential for a deep impact.

To ensure that every step is really understood and drilled into your brain, at the end of every chapter are practical exercises you can complete straight away to help you bring each of the steps to life so you can solve business and real-world problems. Committing some of these ideas onto paper will help you immensely as you go, and you can always return to them after you've read through the whole book if you'd rather not stop to work on exercises.

Nolan Bushnell is an American inventor who started coming up with ideas for video games in the late 1960s and early 1970s. The first game he created with Ted Dabney was Computer Space, a complicated program where spaceships zoomed around a dark night sky trying to shoot aliens and avoid their fire. It was the first commercially available arcade game, and was also extremely difficult to play, meaning the 1500 machines they produced made little money. The pair went back to the drawing board and instead came up with an easier-to-understand game in 1971. It featured a white 'ball' in the screen that bounced back and forth between two 'paddles' that were moved up and down by the two players. They called it Pong and it was an instant success, fuelled by its novelty for people who had never played a video game before. The pair went on to found their own company, Atari, which dominated home gaming and computers for the next decade and a half. 'Everyone who's ever taken a shower has had an idea,' Nolan has said. 'It's the person who gets out of the shower, dries off, and does something about it who makes a difference.'

He's right too. One of the great secrets of creativity is that coming up with ideas is easy. The hard part is shaping them into something with potential, and the most difficult part is bringing the best ones to life. All of us face challenges at work and at home every single day, and when we do, we've got a choice to make. We can either let that problem take control of us, or we can meet it head on and think of creative ways to solve it. That's the power that killer thinking can have to make you more creative, successful, efficient and fulfilled in every part of your life, and that's why I'm so genuinely excited you're about to come on this journey and learn how to unlock your own creativity.

Everything begins with an idea: it's time to start exploring the best ones.

Killer Ideas

How many ideas do we have each day?

Given how fleeting they can be, and how quickly our brains can shift gears from one thing to the next, it's hard for the average person to figure out the answer to that question. For decades scientists have tried to track how many thoughts and ideas we have each day, and they've failed miserably. They often relied on volunteers to describe their own thoughts, which is a self-defeating exercise.

Researchers at Queen's University in Canada made a breakthrough recently when they decided to stop trying to follow what someone was thinking about, and instead measure when the brain activity showed they had moved on to a new thought. Dr Jordan Poppenk and a master's student, Julie Tseng, named each of these a 'thought worm' and published their results in *Nature Communications* in July 2020.[1] 'When a person moves on to a new thought, they create a new thought worm that we can detect with our methods,' said Dr Poppenk, who is the Canada Research Chair in Cognitive Neuroscience.

The most fascinating finding of the research is that based on the number of thought worms they've tracked, they estimate that the average person has around 6,200 thoughts per day.

Just stop and think about that: you have 6,200 thoughts every single day of your life. That's an overwhelming number of things floating in and out of your head trying to get your attention, ranging from minutiae like, Where did I leave my glasses? all the way through to, Why aren't I happier? and How do I solve that big problem at work?

Most of this happens in the background of our minds like the random dripping of thoughts, processing of senses and the internal dialogue no one will ever hear. Among that barrage of information, occasionally lurking between those thousands of fleeting thoughts, is an idea. A golden, precious thought about how something can be done better.

Every idea that's changed the world began when someone grabbed hold of one of those thought worms when it first reared its head, and then didn't let go of it like they did most of the other 6,199.

A lot of the thoughts that bounce around our heads are just noise: recurring reminders, recycled opinions we've absorbed, or a funny video we've just seen on the internet. Then there are the ideas that rise above the rest because they might be a solution to a problem that's been bugging you, or an elegant way of combining two things that could change the way something works.

To help you identify which ideas are worth looking out for and developing into something more, we're going to build a framework that will allow you to test and strengthen any ideas and push them along the scale to greatness. Remember, killer ideas are:

Kind

Impactful

Loved

Lasting

Easy

Repeatable

Let's go through each of these in more detail.

Kind

Kindness isn't a word that's often used in a workplace setting. Kindness can sometimes sound weak, or soft, or too touchy-feely for the thrust and pace of business, right?

I reckon that's bullshit. We've been told for decades that business is a cut-throat, competitive, win-at-all-costs fight against others to claw your way to the top. There are entire TV genres dedicated to people outdoing each other in business by backstabbing in order to become number one.

Kindness is missing from traditional business, and it needs to be more than just a buzzword. The best ideas are sympathetic to the world in which they exist. They are kind to the environment, the supply chain, their customers and staff. And the best part? Kindness is contagious. Stanford University psychologist Jamil Zaki and his colleagues set out to test if seeing other people's good behaviour would inspire people to act in the same positive way.[2] They did this in various ways. The first was to recruit participants to complete a paid study, and at the end give each recruit a one-dollar 'bonus'. They showed them brief overviews of a hundred charities and asked if they wanted to donate any of their bonuses to each of the worthy groups. The participants saw how much other participants had donated, which was, unbeknownst to them, manipulated up and down by the researchers. The result was that people who believed we lived in a generous world where others were donating a high percentage of their bonus donated similarly high amounts. In other words, the kindness of others was contagious.

To test it even further and ensure it wasn't just guilty imitation, they conducted a follow-up study where participants observed other people donating either generously or stingily. They were then told they were moving on to a completely unrelated task where they pretended they had a pen pal. The participants were given a note to read where the pen pal had described their life over the last month, including all of the ups and downs, and then had to write back to them. The researchers found that the participants' letters to their pen pals differed in tone depending on what they had observed earlier. Participants who had watched people donate generously wrote notes that were friendlier, and more empathetic and supportive, compared to the ones from those who had watched people behave greedily. 'Witnessing kindness inspires kindness, causing it to spread like a virus,' wrote Jamil Zaki in *Scientific American*. 'We find that people imitate not only the particulars of positive actions, but also the spirit underlying them. This implies that kindness itself is contagious, and that it can cascade across people, taking on new forms along the way.'

Killer ideas begin with kindness at their core, and spread far and wide outside their original bubble. Ideas that are inherently kind travel around a community, a country and even the world.

Think about the entire ecosystem that surrounds your business, and how kind each aspect is.

Customers: Do you treat them with kindness? Do you listen to them, respond in a timely manner, and take into account their needs ahead of your own?

Environment: How kind is your idea, business or company on the environment? Are you leaving the world in a better state than you found it? Or are you just taking and not replenishing anything else at the other end?

Staff: Are you fair and reasonable with your colleagues? If you keep empathy at the forefront of your decisions, it'll help you make better ones.

Supply chain: How kind are you to people you purchase from? Are you reasonable in your demands from them? Do you consider the entire process?

It must be pointed out that kindness doesn't mean bending over backwards and saying yes to anyone's demands. Kindness can play out in unexpected ways, especially when it comes to other people. Research professor and author Brené Brown writes in *Dare to Lead* that 'Clear is kind. Unclear is unkind',[3] and shows that data reveals most people think they're being kind by avoiding clarity, when the opposite is actually true. Some things might not seem kind at first glance, but you have to take into account the bigger picture and how it affects everyone.

Google has a position called a Chief Innovation Evangelist. It's a strange title with a very worthy job description. It's their job to encourage people, both inside and outside of Google, to pursue radically new ideas, think with an innovation mindset and figure out what needs to change in current workplaces to get there.[4] The current Chief Innovation Evangelist, Frederik Pferdt, says the skill that will be needed most in the future is empathy.[5] 'Practising empathy every day as a business leader, for example, helps you understand what your employees need and what your immediate team actually needs right now. So, putting yourself into their situation, to really understand how they really think and feel, helps you come up with better solutions for your employees.'

If you begin with empathy, clarity and kindness as the core motivators for an idea, you'll be well on your way to creating a contagious idea that can build its own momentum and really catch on.

Impactful

Killer ideas have serious impact. They exist to fulfil a clear purpose that is obvious to everyone involved. Every killer idea has a clear Impact Statement, a concept I explored in detail in *Cult Status*. As a quick refresher, an Impact Statement lays out exactly the effect you want to have on the people who use your service or product. An Impact Statement is different from a goal. A business goal is generally a number to reach, like 'sell one thousand computers' or 'call one thousand people'. An Impact Statement is also different from a Mission Statement. A Mission Statement describes your purpose or mission. It's the reason that you exist, the *what?* of your company. An Impact Statement is the *so what?* of your company. If you fulfil your mission, then what effect is that going to have? If you want to learn more about Impact Statements, head to timduggan.com.au.

Killer ideas are super impactful, with effects that are often felt in multiple communities. Anyone can think of an idea that is good, but a truly impactful idea *does* good. Killer ideas exist for a very specific reason: to solve a problem that's easily understood by everyone who hears the idea.

The best ideas in the world have a clear purpose beyond just making money. Of course, some of the best ideas have truly impressive revenue streams, but that is not their sole reason for being. The reason they resonate so much is because their purpose is clearly understood by consumers who identify strongly with it.

A killer idea is a living, breathing organism that moves on a journey from good to great to killer. When an idea connects with an audience, it gets taken on by them and becomes part of their stories as well. That allows the idea to grow and change and have a strong impact over a long period of time.

It can be overwhelming to think you need to come up with ideas that will be so earth-shatteringly good they will change *everything*. If you've got huge ambitions, then by all means go for gold and I won't get in your way. But not everyone has the same approach, and some ideas can be measured by how deeply the results are felt by a targeted number of people instead. Remember that every successful creative idea starts small, and with the right refinement, tenacity and adaptation you can build the quality and quantity of your impact.

Loved

Killer ideas aren't just liked, they are absolutely loved. There's a big difference between liking something and absolutely loving it, and that's the difference between a good idea and a great one. When an idea is really adored, it's welcomed into people's lives.

There are three main reasons people fall in love with an idea:

- they identify strongly with the purpose of what it's aiming to do;
- the idea helps people express who they are; and/or
- it makes them feel better about themselves.

Some of the best ideas tick all of those boxes simultaneously, and if you can tap into just one of those deep connectors to create a business or movement that makes someone feel seen, it's a very powerful foundation for long-term success.

Jay Coen Gilbert is the co-founder of the B Corp movement, a coalition of businesses that meets the highest standards of verified social and environmental performance and accountability in balancing profit and purpose together. 'An idea will take on a life of its own if people love doing it,' he says. 'I would argue that love is the most important form of value. If someone makes me feel good, I want to spend more time with them because it feels good to feel good.'

When something is loved, it can help an idea transcend all the noise and be deeply felt by the people who need it. Think right now about someone you really love (shout-out to my husband Ben, who I'm thinking of right at this moment). When you are deeply in love with someone, you don't sweat the small stuff but you do concentrate on the bigger picture. They might annoy you occasionally, or you have an argument, or they do something that pisses you off (and vice versa) – but in the end it doesn't mean much; they are just temporary emotions that get overridden by a deeper gratitude when you really love someone. It's the same with a killer idea. Any small defects in a product, the execution or communication, can all be forgiven if a customer is in love with the idea behind it and all it stands for.

Loved ideas spread far because customers become enthusiastic advocates for them, organically telling others and helping amplify word-of-mouth marketing. The goal of any business or movement is to be loved and appreciated.

Lasting

Killer ideas have staying power. They are living beasts that evolve along with the moment, shifting and morphing to react to feedback and what the current situation demands of them. The best ideas are ones that are fluid and responsive and that will evolve and last for a long time.

Don't be afraid if an idea changes as more people get involved, or as the world around you changes. Nothing is set in stone, and the environment and world around us are constantly moving. The best ideas are vigorously tested by lots of different people, and grow stronger with each iteration. They're flexible and they adapt to the needs of whoever is using them at the time.

The reason the best ideas last so long is because they often hook into a movement that's bigger than just them. Launching your idea on the back of a rising tide will give it the best chance of riding the wave for a long time. Movements have momentum, and they allow an idea to gather a greater speed than if it were going against a trend.

To build an idea that lasts, you need to respond to feedback and adapt to it. There's a big difference between listening and hearing, and the best developers of ideas take note which parts of customer feedback should be acted upon.

A truly great idea can last for years, even decades, as it taps into a timeless truth. An idea that stands the test of time does so because it gives ongoing value to its audience. The value might be financial, fun or bringing meaning to their lives, but whatever it is, the value exchange means the idea stays around for a long time.

Brilliant ideas are also lasting, because they have reliable revenue models built around them that generate income for everyone involved. The best ideas in the world can easily lose people's attention if they are not financially sustainable.

Of course, every idea has its day. Good ideas last a while, and great ideas even longer. But killer ideas can become part of the fabric of society such that they will outlast their founders, stretching and growing with each new generation.

Easy

A killer idea is a simple one. It's uncomplicated, straightforward and easily understood in just a sentence. If you can't break it down and explain it easily to an eight-year-old, it's probably not a killer idea.

Simplicity is often overlooked. The greatest ideas in the world are very basic at their core, broken down into key elements. Ease of understanding is part of the reason they are able to spread beyond language and geographical boundaries. If you really want to test a killer idea, see how easily it translates in another culture. If it can cross over into another city, state or country with the same level of impact and understanding, you're onto a good thing.

The simplicity of an idea is directly related to how far it spreads. If it takes you a few tortured minutes to describe how something works, how can you expect it to be passed on to another person? In his seminal book *Simplicity*, philosopher Edward de Bono writes that in order to be most creative we must break the complex down into manageable and recognisable parts (he also argues with a straight face that the word 'simplifying' is way too complicated and should be replaced with the much easier 'simping').

You might have the best idea in the world, but if no one else can understand it because it's too complicated, it's useless. There is a real artform to brutally simplifying an idea to its core, and it's something you'll learn in reading this book.

Repeatable

Killer ideas create their own momentum to keep them self-sustaining in perpetuity. They are easily able to be repeated over and over, each time gaining new audiences who love them and pass them on to more people. A killer idea is contagious, powered by its own brilliance.

Think back to an idea you really thought was amazing. You might have then told someone else, lighting up with enthusiasm about it, watching their reaction as you explain the idea. Like a chain, this can go on and on, fuelled only by the power of creativity behind a killer idea. The best ideas in the world will engender their own vitality based on their own quality.

Many of us get fired up when we hear a great idea and want to tell others about it. If you can harness that energy, and give people a story they can pass on, it becomes repeatable. Most people want to spread goodness, and killer ideas that tap into making the world a slightly better place, or having a positive impact, become their own renewable energy source and get repeated over and over, winning new fans each time.

The killer thinking you'll learn in this book can help you generate, refine and execute ideas that are kind, impactful, loved, lasting, easy and repeatable. These descriptors don't live in a vacuum, and there is some overlap between them. For example, if an idea is kind to its community, that will help build love for it. If an idea is easy to understand, it's more likely to be repeated. If an idea has genuine impact, it's likely to last for a long time. The beauty of the KILLER framework is that each of the parts interplays with the others in unique ways to form super strong, solid ideas that work.

Not every idea in this book is a killer idea. Some of them are just smart, or illustrative, or interesting, but once you know what to look for, you can see examples of killer thinking everywhere to help inspire you with your own.

They can be broken down into two main types, amazing businesses and powerful movements, with some exceptional ones straddling both. Here are some examples of how killer thinking can be used in business.

reCAPTCHA

You know the 'human' test when you're logging in to something that asks you to decipher a series of random letters to prove you're not a robot? Those ten seconds add up to two billion wasted seconds of time every day, a problem that computer scientist Luis von Ahn solved in 2007 by launching reCaptcha. Every time you do one of those tests, you are actually unknowingly helping to digitise and translate text that computers can't decipher, using the collective power of billions of people, one log-in at a time. reCaptcha helped the *New York Times* digitise 129 years' worth of articles in 24 months,[6] and Luis later used similar thinking to launch Duolingo, now the most downloaded education app in the world, which teaches over 40 million people a month another language.

Tony's Chocolonely

Dutch journalist Teun van de Keuken discovered a dirty little secret in 2002: a lot of mass-produced chocolate made at the time was produced on cocoa plantations that used slave labour. Millions of children in West Africa were forced to work without pay to keep up with global demand. Teun first started making TV programs about the issue, and then decided to use the tools of business to create a solution. He launched Tony's Chocolonely in 2005 and sold 20,000 bars in two days; the company is now one of the largest chocolate manufacturers in the Netherlands, providing better prices and slave-free working conditions to more than 7,000 farmers.[7]

Great Wrap

Kitchen cling wrap can be made from a variety of plastics, but the most popular material is polyvinyl chloride (PVC); it's hard to recycle and mainly ends up in landfill. With the average Australian family going through 24 rolls of plastic wrap every year, it's a serious issue. Husband-and-wife team Jordy and Julia Kay were sick of this problem, so they spent years perfecting a recipe for a new type of cling film called Great Wrap. Designed to cater to consumers and businesses that need pallet wrapping but want an environmentally sustainable solution, their latest formula is made by diverting food waste from landfill and converting it into the main raw ingredient. Their product breaks down into carbon and water in a compost pile; this is just the start of a revolution in minimising plastic pollution.

Fable

The origin story of this business sounds like a fable: two vegetarians, a celebrity chef and a mushroom geek go for a walk in the woods... but when Michael Fox, Chris McLoghlin and Jim Fuller convinced Heston Blumenthal to try some of their 'meaty'-flavoured mushrooms, a food products company was born. Fable uses the dense, fleshy fibres and umami flavours of shiitake mushrooms as the basis for meat alternatives that are winning fans all around the globe, and helping to make it easier for people to transition to plant-based foods – a diet that's way better for the environment.

Canva

Launched in 2013 by Melanie Perkins, Cliff Obrecht and Cameron Adams, Canva is the powerhouse online design and publishing tool with a mission to empower everyone in the world to design anything and publish anywhere. For decades, design software had been complicated and burdensome. You need to take a course just to understand how to use programs like Photoshop, and they're damn expensive too. Canva has a lofty aim to democratise graphic design, and in the process has become one of the world's most valuable privately owned companies. Melanie and Cliff are on a path to donating the vast majority of their equity in Canva, around 30 per cent, to philanthropy, in a move that reflects the inherent kindness built into not just the idea that lowers the barriers to good design, but also their entire business approach.

Bardee

This business, founded in 2019, is built off the back of insects. Architect Phoebe Gardner and entomologist Alex Arnold are the custodians of over one billion black soldier flies housed in a vertical farming system in their Melbourne warehouse. Phoebe and Alex bring food waste from restaurants, shopping centres and local businesses to the fly larvae, which convert the waste into insect protein that can be used in products like fertiliser and cattle feed. This naturally occurring process can recover 90 per cent of the nutrients that are normally thrown away at a rate that's ten times faster than commercial composting,[8] with enormous potential at scale.

Applying killer thinking can help you create a successful business with real staying power. Here are some examples of killer thinking in social movements that exist for a greater purpose than just making money, even if they do often generate revenue. Ideas like these have traditionally been called 'non-profits', but a better name for them is for-impact or for-purpose businesses or movements, as they exist to fulfil a specific aim.

La Ciclovía

Every Sunday the Colombian capital of Bogotá shuts down 120 kilometres of its streets to cars – the roads are handed over to more than two million cyclists, runners, children and walkers every weekend. Started in 1974 by cycling enthusiast Jaime Ortiz Mariño and his friends, a version of La Ciclovía (pronounced 'seek-low-vee-ah') is repeated in over 400 cities all over the world, from Belgium to San Francisco. It helps citizens re-imagine what it means to share the streets, with endless liveability improvements in the cities in which it occurs.

The Big Issue

Launched in 1991 as a direct response to the large number of rough sleepers on the streets of London, *The Big Issue* turns its vendors into micro-entrepreneurs by giving them an opportunity to earn an income selling magazines directly to the public and keep the profit themselves. This clever twist on the traditional magazine distribution model has helped over 92,000 vendors earn GBP £115 million in the UK over the past 25 years, and has inspired over 100 similar magazines in 35 countries around the world.

Change for Good

When you get on the plane to fly from one country to the next, everyone always has those stray coins that instantly become useless until the next time you return (if you even do). In 1987, for-impact charity UNICEF came up with a killer idea called Change for Good. They convinced a bunch of airlines to ask the cabin crew to collect the unused coins and donate them to UNICEF's work. Since then, this initiative has raised over US$140 million that would have otherwise been thrown out or sat inside people's cupboards collecting dust.

The Bread & Butter Project

Paul Allam and his wife Jessica Grynberg co-founded the beloved Sydney institution Bourke Street Bakery in 2004. When they visited an orphanage on the border of Thailand and Myanmar a few years later, they spent some of their time teaching the women how to bake bread to help support themselves and their community. After returning home they were inspired to start the Bread & Butter Project, a social-enterprise bakery that invests 100 per cent of its profits towards training and employment opportunities for refugees and asylum seekers in Sydney. Every delicious slice of bread helps to educate the next generation of bakers, and it's now stocked on the shelves of major supermarkets.

The Moser Lamp

In 2002, a Brazilian mechanic named Alfredo Moser had a simple light-bulb idea: he filled an empty plastic bottle with water, added two capfuls of bleach to stop the water turning green and inserted it through the ceiling and roof of his simple home. Using the refraction of sunlight through the water in the bottle into the room below, he had just created an inexpensive, recycled homemade light that was as bright as a 40- to 60-watt electric bulb during the day. His idea spread quickly throughout developing countries and is estimated to now be installed in millions of homes. Moser never patented his idea or made any money from it, content that its impact was more important than money. He brought to life an idea that's cheap, effective and simple.

OzHarvest

Ronni Kahn was an events organiser who couldn't help but notice the huge volume of food being thrown away at the end of her events. She came up with a simple solution to a glaring problem: she bought a van to start rescuing food that was about to be discarded and deliver it to local charities. Ronni's little idea grew quickly, and today OzHarvest has a fleet of bright yellow vans that roam Australia collecting surplus food from cafes, restaurants, airlines and hotels. Their workers turn the surplus into meals that over 1,600 charities share with people in need. Since the organisation started out of Ronni's van in 2004, they have now made over 190 million delicious and nutritious meals out of good-quality surplus food that was destined for the garbage bin.[9]

These are just a taste of some examples of killer thinking on a grand scale. It doesn't matter if you want to build the next business that will change millions of people's lives, or just crack a problem that's been bugging you for a long time. The same thinking can be applied to all ideas, big or small.

The Eight Steps you're about to learn are intended to be a guide to help you navigate all of the jumbled thoughts that can overwhelm you when you decide it's time to get creative. If you know you want a brilliant idea to help you kick some goals, but don't know exactly where to start, you've come to the right place.

Step 1:
Be Your Problem's Therapist

Be your problem's therapist

A woodsman was once asked, 'What would you do if you had just five minutes to chop down a tree?' He answered, 'I would spend the first two and a half minutes sharpening my axe.'

Anonymous

Be Your Problem's Therapist

B ritish Columbia is the westernmost province of Canada, bookended by the Pacific coastline on the west and rugged mountain ranges like the Canadian Rockies in the east. It's also the home of dozens of 7-11 convenience stores, most of them dotted around major cities like Vancouver.

In the mid 1980s a number of these stores had a problem. Drawn like moths to the fluorescent lights, groups of young people were hanging out in the car parks in front of the 7-11s – not to do much of anything except sit together on the hoods of their cars late into the night listening to music and catching up. It wasn't a problem unique to 7-11s, but their car parks were quickly becoming the main after-hours locations for young people to meet up and pass the time. It didn't take long for these spontaneous, loud parties to begin to affect 7-11's evening trade and the comfort of other customers coming in.

Before they could solve this problem, 7-11 needed to understand everything about it. So they convened a group that could look at the issue from every angle. It wasn't just the usual team of managers and senior leaders; they consulted with young people in their company, recruited staff members who dealt with the kids every day and even included a psychologist as part of the problem-solving team so they could really get to the bottom of why this was occurring.

The group spent hours interrogating, questioning and challenging their preconceived ideas. With lots of different perspectives in the room, they defined the problem and acted out various creative ways of trying to solve it. One of their ideas was to increase the number and hours of security in front of each store, but that was quickly shelved as an expensive exercise that might just antagonise the crowds, leading to a deteriorating outcome. Another option was to close the stores earlier, but that would just inconvenience their customers and lead to less revenue. Someone else suggested they could try turning off the outdoor car park lights, but that was also shelved due to safety concerns.

Then someone in the room, who had spent a lot of time trying to put themselves in the shoes of the gathering young people, came up with a left-field suggestion: Forget confrontation or additional security, their solution would cost nothing to execute, was non-violent and extremely easy for other stores to copy. If they wanted the young people to move on from the front of their stores, why don't they just play classical music in the car park?

The idea was deceptively simple, and came from a deep understanding that young people wanted to hang out somewhere 'cool' with their friends, and didn't want to listen to classical or 'easy listening' music that would be seen as daggy and get in the way of their conversations. The idea that came from this creative session was immediately trialled in ten stores in British Columbia in 1985.

To everyone's surprise, it worked. The teens who arrived every night to catch up with their friends couldn't stand listening to 'uncool' music and stopped hanging out in the 7-11 car parks. The creative solution was then repeated in 150 more stores across the United States and Canada. It was the start of a trend that's been executed in train stations, bus stops, museums and car parks worldwide.

In 2001, police in West Palm Beach in Florida began playing music by Beethoven, Bach and Mozart at an intersection that was notorious for crime. 'The troubled corner showed marked improvement with the launch of programmed classical music there,' wrote author Lily Hirsch, 'despite a brief pause of three weeks after vandals removed speaker wires and destroyed the building's electrical meter.'[10]

In the Sydney suburb of Rockdale in 2006, the local council cheekily referred to it as the Manilow Method because they chose to play Barry Manilow's greatest hits through a loudspeaker in a car park every Friday and Saturday night from nine pm. 'Barry's our secret weapon,' the council's deputy mayor said.[11] Even though it had been successful in thousands of locations since its first incarnation in 7-11 car parks, the only person who doubted this technique would work was Barry Manilow himself. When asked about it, Manilow wondered whether it might actually have the opposite effect. 'What if this actually attracts more hoodlums? What if it puts smiles on their faces?' he said.[12] 'Have they thought that these hoodlums might like my music? What if some of them began to sing along to "Can't Smile Without You"? Or lit candles when "I Write the Songs" was played? Or, heaven forbid, danced around to the infectious beat of "Copacabana"?' Despite Manilow's wry observations, the idea worked just as well in Sydney in 2006 as it did in British Columbia in 1985. The final word came from the Rockdale council, who cheerily reported that 'The youths have now left the area.'

There are obvious questions to be asked here around the value of just displacing young people from certain areas where authorities don't want them to linger, but as far as creative solutions go, it was a simple one. Part of its success was that it got under the hood of the problem and really understood the reasons people hang out together, and theorising that trying to look 'cool' to your friends isn't as effortless when Barry Manilow is crooning away in the background.

To find a right solution you need to ensure you're solving the right problem. Every problem has a nucleus to it: a bare truth that exists right at its very centre. Jeff Goodby and Rich Silverstein, the founders of the legendary advertising agency Goodby Silverstein & Partners, say that you should 'be the problem's therapist',[13] and it's a phrase I love. Every creative idea is the solution to a problem, and if you want to come up with a killer idea, you need to know your problem inside out, better than anyone else. Studies have even found that better thinkers spend more time upfront planning out exactly what the problem is than poor reasoners.[14] You need to prod and probe to try to really understand a problem if you're going to even think about solving it.

The Rule of Thirds

I'm not a psychic, but I reckon I'd be able to recount exactly how your last creative ideation session at work went. This isn't due to any particular mind-reading ability on my behalf, but mainly thanks to experience. I've participated in hundreds of group creative sessions over the years, from small affairs with just two of us bouncing ideas back and forth over a quick meal, to formal meetings run by international creative agencies and multi-day conferences at global retreats held in grand hotel ballrooms.

Tell me if this sounds familiar: you're sitting at your office desk or in front of your computer at home when all of a sudden an email pops up in your inbox: *Brainstorm, Thursday 2pm*. That's it. Not much context around what it's about, what you're trying to achieve or how you can prepare for it.

You turn up at the office boardroom or log on to the Zoom call at two pm on Thursday to find several other people sitting around waiting for the organiser to tell them what the meeting is about. 'OK,' they begin, 'we need to come up with some creative ideas on how we can solve this problem. Who's got some?'

If I tasked you to come up with the worst possible way of being creative, you'd probably come up with a brainstorm. Put an hour-long meeting into people's diaries, gather a group of varying experience around a boardroom table, and then demand that they come up with some ideas on the spot with the clock ticking.

It's a recipe for disaster, right? And here's the harsh truth: brainstorms suck.

When a brainstorm doesn't come up with any good ideas, it's easy to lay the blame at the feet of the people in the room. Maybe we didn't get the right team together, you might hear. Or maybe it was because Jenny, the creative thinker of the group, wasn't there. Or maybe it was too late in the day. Or was it too early?

I'm here to tell you that it's not due to a lack of creativity in the room: it's because brainstorms are generally a terrible way of being creative that have somehow seeped into modern corporate culture and become deeply engrained in how we think about ideas. We'll spend some more time in Step 3 going over the history of brainstorms, and how we can revolutionise them for the modern workplace.

Despite what you might think, every single person in the world is creative, and harnessing the right hemisphere of your brain to find unique solutions to problems is the most important skill you're going to need in the workplace of tomorrow.

I am a big believer in the inherent creativity inside all of us. As kids it's nurtured and encouraged in us, when we were given crayons, paper, pipe cleaners and Play-Doh and told to make whatever is inside our head. Some of my fondest childhood memories are of hours spent assembling the new Lego village, or forcing my siblings to help me record radio plays on cassette tapes, complete with sound effects and character voices – basically a crude prototype of a podcast.

Creativity is deeply encouraged and cultivated in children. But then what happens? 'Everyone is given a box of crayons in kindergarten,' wrote author Hugh MacLeod in his book *Ignore Everything: and 39 Other Keys to Creativity*. 'Then when you hit puberty they take the crayons away and replace them with dry, uninspiring books on algebra, history, etc. Being suddenly hit years later with the "creative bug" is just a wee voice telling you, "I'd like my crayons back, please."'[15]

When we enter our teenage years, it's not so cool any more to spend hours creating. Some of us retreat inside our own heads when we become young adults to try to figure out how the world works, while others are drawn to the glowing distraction of the digital world that sucks us into addiction. Whatever causes it, most of us give up on creativity after that. A few lucky people might become 'creatives' for their jobs, or 'artists' in some way, and that's about it. At least, that's the case until a brainstorm meeting invite lands in our email calendar.

There's a misguided belief that only a small portion of people are creative. However, some of the most creative people are the ones you'd least suspect of imagination or innovative resourcefulness. Creativity is the ability to come up with new, useful ideas, and that's something anyone can do.

Don't think you are creative? Don't worry. Research by Simone M Ritter and Nel Mostert published in the *Journal of Cognitive Enhancement* showed that creative potential can be facilitated with training.[16] In fact, they believe that even just one short single training session (approximately one and a half hours) on the cognitive skills needed for creativity improved performance on a variety of well-validated measures. Just one 90-minute session! Now imagine the boost in creative ability you'll have by the time you get to the end of this book!

The main reasons brainstorms fail is that they're just not in tune with how the creative process works. To unlock creativity that's been stifled by modern life, you need to understand the difference between divergent and convergent thinking.

Divergent thinking is the ability to generate lots of different ideas. Convergent thinking is sifting through all those ideas to choose the most promising ones that you could actually do. They are both required when you come up with ideas, and in order to be creative you need to switch between both of those ways of thinking.

43

Divergent thinking	Convergent thinking
Generating lots of ideas	Choosing the best ideas
Uses imagination	Uses logic
Creating choices	Making choices
Lateral	Literal
Asking questions	Answering questions
Free flowing	Targeted

The interplay between these two types of thinking is very important. Professor Mark A Runco, the founder of the *Creativity Research Journal*, believes that most people focus on the wrong thing.[17] We're taught to believe there is often one single, correct answer to our problems. 'However,' he says, 'most complex and ill-defined questions don't have one single, correct answer. To successfully deal with problems and challenges in our complex and fast-changing world, we have to rely on and trigger our divergent thinking skills.'

Now, I want you to return to your most recent brainstorming session, or any time when you last gathered with other people for a creative idea-generating session. It might have been at work, at university, on Zoom, in a boardroom or it could even have been just a bunch of friends sitting around. A typical creative session has three main components:

Understanding the problem: Getting to the crux of what you're trying to solve.

Individual ideas: Time spent coming up with ideas by yourself.

Group ideas: Time spent as a group coming up with solutions collectively.

If I were a fly on the wall inside a workplace brainstorming session and divided up the amount of time spent on each of those tasks, I would bet money that most would look something like this:

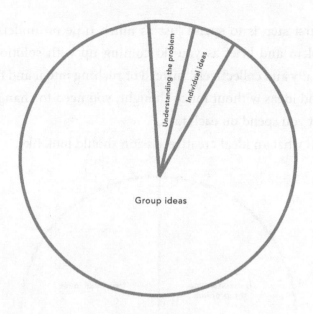

Understanding the problem

Individual ideas

Group ideas

It's not unusual to spend hours going round in circles with little to show for it at the end but a whiteboard covered with random scribbled words. Sometimes you might get lucky, but group solutions tend to be inconsistent and dominated by loud voices, and they can easily go down long, distracting paths unless they are well moderated.

That's the bad news out of the way. The good news is that based on hundreds of hours spent in creative sessions, studying dozens of research papers, speaking to countless people and years of experimentation, I've learnt there *are* better ways of thinking about creativity and of coming up with solutions to some of the most vexing global problems, as well as the micro solutions that can make our lives that tiny bit better.

I do have to point out at this moment, however, that creativity is not something with a 100 per cent hit rate – it's way messier and more unpredictable than that – but following each of the steps in this book will give you a better chance of coming up with your own killer idea, and then bringing it to life.

The first step is to spend just as much time on understanding the problem and brief as you do coming up with solutions, both individually and collectively. Instead of rushing into it and throwing away good ideas without much thought, you need to change up the ratio that you spend on each task.

This is what an ideal creative session should look like:

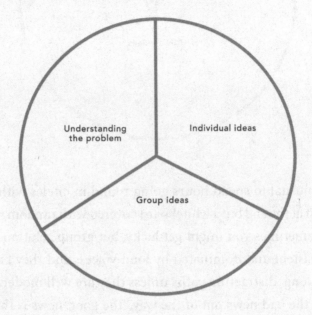

To really understand every inch of a problem you should use the rough rule of thirds.

One third of the time: Understanding the problem and brief.

One third of the time: Coming up with individual solutions.

One third of the time: Coming up with group solutions.

By giving as much time to knowing a problem from all angles as you do to trying to solve it, you can avoid a lot of mistakes. And the best way to do that? Write everything you need to know down into a killer brief.

Nail the Brief

A creative brief is the starting point to explore all of the possible solutions to the problem you're trying to solve. If it's too narrow in its remit, it restricts where you can go, and if it's too wide, there will be simply too many paths to go down that will waste time before you come up with your ideas.

Even if you don't think you need a brief, you will get something out of just running through the exercise of putting one together and writing it down on paper. It will force you to think more deeply about what you're trying to do, and allow you to easily communicate what you're trying to do with lots of people at once. Writing a good brief is wonderfully clarifying and makes you confront some of your preconceived notions about your problem.

You should always start with a clear brief if you want to come up with something new. It could be a product or business idea, or to figure out what to name something, or to pressure-test your process, or to come up with a different workflow. A clear brief can help to solve pretty much anything that you can think of, in both workplace and personal settings.

Now, don't get overwhelmed by trying to cover every aspect of the problem, because an ideal brief is tight and succinct, and should not be much longer than one page. That way it's easily digestible by everyone, it ensures all stakeholders and participants really understand the problem and, again, it provides a springboard for the creative process. Even if you're trying to come up with a killer idea by yourself, the act of writing a brief can help you see the solution more easily than if you don't have one. Committing it to paper is all part of the creative process, and you can sometimes see possible solutions underneath the details as you research to try to understand your issue.

There are literally hundreds of variations on the creative brief, but a great brief has just six core elements that can be expressed on a single page. This is your chance to really understand every inch of what you're trying to solve with a creative idea, and each of these elements will help set you up on the path to creating a killer idea.

The core elements are:

1. Problem
2. Audience
3. Objective
4. Insight
5. Essentials
6. Actions

1. Problem

Every brief should have a problem it's trying to solve. If not, then what *are* you trying to do? It could be that sales are down, a new competitor is joining the market, or you just don't have something that you need.

You have to be brutally honest at this stage, and understand there are no sacred cows when you are coming up with a true problem. Sure, it might hurt someone's feelings to, for example, point out an inefficiency or lack in a system or organisation they're proud of, but you need to get to the root cause of an issue. A problem should be expressed as succinctly as you can. Here are some examples of different types of problems.

Societal problem: *Kids are spending too much time on their phones and not enough time playing with their friends in the real world.*

Business problem: *The average consumer has around 100 different passwords that they're trying to remember in order to log in to different services they use.*

Product problem: *Our widget was launched 15 years ago, but it's now outdated and clumsy to use compared with other products on the market.*

Marketing problem: *Lawyers have informed us that the title of our project is too similar to an existing trademark, so we need to change it within the next month.*

There are an infinite number of problems and they will vary greatly depending on what you're trying to solve. Every single business and person has problems, so it's not hard to find one you want to solve. Summarise your problem as neatly as you can so anyone reading the creative brief can understand it.

2. Audience

Every idea needs an audience. It doesn't matter if you're trying to think more creatively about a work project with an audience of one person, or come up with a business idea with an audience of millions of people: clearly define who it is you're aiming for.

A common mistake is to say 'it's everyone', but that's really just a cop-out. The more specific you can be, the better the solution. Don't just say it's for 'all people aged over 18' – be as specific as possible. A good target market includes both demographic (who they are) and psychographic (what they do) details.

Here are some examples of tightly developed target audiences:

Target market: *Young males aged 18 to 24 who live in metro cities. They've recently finished studying and have started their first job, and they don't mind putting in long hours to try to show their bosses they are hard workers.*

Target market: *First-time parents aged 30 to 34 who live in regional areas. They have a strong family support network who help them navigate the pressure of how to deal with a newborn, but they feel they have no idea if they are parenting the right way or not.*

Of course, you can go a bit wild here with the target market if you have more information. This should be based on customer data, research or insights you already have. When you're writing the creative brief, getting the target market right is very important, as it will direct the tone and scope of your solution. This is the time for you and others to critically review whether you actually have the right target. One common mistake is aiming for an idealised audience when the reality of who actually buys a product is different. Don't go for what you wish you had, go with the reality.

Don't just focus on the demographic details of your potential audience, or you could go wrong. If, for example, I asked you to focus on a specific audience of men born in 1948 who were raised in the UK, had been married twice, lived in a castle and were wealthy and famous, who immediately comes to mind? The fact this targeted demographic covers both Prince Charles *and* Ozzy Osborne should show you the danger in just listing biographical attributes.

It's helpful, if you can, to actually name and personify your bullseye market. Narrow it down so much it's an actual person for you to talk to. What's her name? Where does she live? What does she dream about? Go wild in creating your persona.

At Junkee Media we had a bullseye persona for every media title that we published, and it was a useful prism through which to measure an initiative to ensure we had the right approach. Each of our titles had a specific person – complete with a name, age, what they liked to do and how they spent their spare time – and we would run content ideas past them to see if that specific person would like it.

Take AWOL, our travel title launched in partnership with Qantas in 2014 to inspire young Australians to travel the world. Before we even wrote our first piece of content we created two fictional ideal people, one called 'Ben' and the other 'Chloe', and an entire fantasy world they lived in. Ben was a confident traveller who loved nothing more than strapping on his backpack and heading off to undiscovered places so he could photograph and share them with his friends and family back home. Chloe preferred to travel with a small group of friends, sharing their adventures and posting holiday sunsets on Instagram. The idea for every piece of content we created, from travel guides to explainer videos, was put through the filter of these two people. If a writer pitched a story we didn't think Ben or Chloe was going to read and share with their friends, we'd tweak it or try another angle. The personas became a very useful lens to focus everyone's attention on the same target audience.

Elizabeth Gilbert, the bestselling author of *Eat, Pray, Love* and *Big Magic*, advises any budding writers that the best thing they can do is to keep that picture of their one person in their heads as they write. 'Tell your story TO someone,' she writes.[18] 'Pick one person you love or admire or want to connect with, and write the whole thing directly to them – like you're writing a letter. This will bring forth your natural voice.'

If you can narrow your target market down to a single persona, you're already halfway to getting the brief right and understanding the problem.

3. Objective

What is the business, marketing or personal aim that you're trying to achieve? Is there a goal to help society, sell more products, create something new, or just to be creative for the sake of it?

Think of the objective as the opposite to your problem. If you were able to solve it, what would you hope to achieve? Try to keep your objective as CALM as you can. CALM stands for Clear, Achievable, Living and Measurable:

Clear: It should be so clear and concise that an eight-year-old would understand it.

Achievable: We all love to aim high, but make sure you set realistic achievements if all goes to plan.

Living: The objective should be a living, breathing organism that constantly evolves. It can be updated monthly or quarterly if it's an ongoing problem.

Measurable: How are you going to tell if your solution has succeeded or not?

4. Insight

It's necessary to keep stripping away the layers of a problem until you get to the very nucleus of it: doing so gives you insight into what's needed.

The best insights come from observing the problem. This could be from noting key pain points that occur in a particular process among different people, or by asking people what they're thinking about a product or social issue. It might also come from research into an audience that helps you uncover the reasons behind a problem.

What makes a great insight is that it's usually a couple of layers deeper than just the surface. An insight is a peek into human behaviour that people might not realise is a truth until they're told about it. It shouldn't be based just on a hunch, and should be backed up by some form of objective information: research studies, surveys, statistics, facts or information that you know.

If you base your solution on just a hunch without anything to back it up, you *might* end up with a good solution if you're lucky, but you're more likely to waste time, energy, resources and creativity trying to find a solution for a problem that doesn't exist outside your own head. This is where biases and stereotypes can lead you astray. To avoid this, base your 'truth' on objective data – even if colleagues or friends agree with your perspective. Just because *you* all feel the same way doesn't mean that's how other humans think.

A common problem in corporate creative problem-solving is 'brand myopia'. This is short-sightedness caused by being so close to something that you can't see it in the same way as a consumer can. If you spend all day every day living and breathing a brand or business, you are probably the worst people to judge what an average consumer is thinking. Use research and third parties to help you see things through other people's eyes.

5. Essentials

What are the boxes this solution *must* tick if it's going to work? This part of the brief will become especially important once you've completed your divergent thinking and come up with lots of ideas, and then you begin to use convergent thinking to narrow them down to the best one. What are the must-have principles you'll use to ensure it's the right fit for your problem?

In Step 5 you will learn how to filter your ideas, taking the essential principles in the KILLER filter (kind, impactful, loved, lasting, easy and repeatable) and using them to determine which ideas should be explored more, and which ones don't pass the test. You should add your own list of what is essential to this as well.

This will vary for every idea, so think about what is truly essential for a potential solution. Most of these can be derived from limitations you have, or rules that must be followed.

Some examples of essentials that could be include in a brief are:

- needs to be done for under $1,000;
- the idea has to work on Zoom;
- the final product must work in multiple languages;
- should be created using recyclable materials; or
- the solution needs to fit into the back of a car.

For the last six years I've been a proud board member of the Griffin Theatre Company, a mighty little troupe that's recognised as one of the most creative in Australia. Part of that is because its home theatre is a rough and unpretentious place that seats only 105 people on bench seats. Converted from a nineteenth-century stable, this tiny space helps fuel new ways of tackling distinct and original Australian stories. Many of the country's most beloved and celebrated artists, such as actor Cate Blanchett and playwright Michael Gow, began their careers figuring out the best way to use the cramped triangular stage of Griffin's SBW Stables Theatre to best effect. 'Griffin's constraints don't ever really hinder me, they only help,' says Artistic Director Declan Greene. 'You can't approach the theatre imagining that you're going to make it conform to your idea, because there are just very hard limits to what it can offer you. For instance, if you write a play that relies on a heart-wrenching third-last scene where the family gather around Grandma dying in her hospital bed... Sorry, but it's just not going to happen. At Griffin we can't get a big object, like a hospital bed, onstage and then offstage again. There's literally no room backstage to store it! So either that bed is onstage for the whole play, or you need to figure out a whole other way for Grandma to die.' By reframing constraints as essentials, limitations can become an opportunity rather than an obstacle to help fuel your creativity.

6. Action

The final component of really understanding a problem is clarifying what you would like people to do if there was a solution to it. What is the clear Call to Action (CTA)? The best ideas in the world have an obvious CTA: a clear action you want someone to take helps an idea spread and become renewable, powered by its own energy.

The Call to Action should be specific rather than abstract, and ideally make people feel that performing the action will make a real difference. This is how many social movements and great ideas are able to spread easily through and between communities. If the audience feels their action is going to help other people, they are more likely to perform it, and the more people who see it, the further potential it has to spread.

What you want someone to do might be small, like just becoming aware of your topic, or massive, like spending millions of dollars on something you are selling. Whatever it is, keep it simple and actionable.

These are the six core components of a great brief, and you should aim to spend at least one third of your time as a group making sure everyone is across them before you dive into the fun part of generating ideas.

Vince Frost, the founder of creative agency Frost*collective, says one of the most important parts of creativity is challenging every word of the brief to ensure everyone truly understands it. 'I like challenges and I like questioning the challenges,' he says. 'I don't just accept the brief as it is. I want to understand, is this the right brief? Have they thought this through or have I missed something?... If you just take it on as it is and don't question it, you're really doing a disservice to yourself and to the opportunity... You need to interrogate it, chat about it, question it, work on it, improve it.'

When Vince first began working as a young graphic designer, he used to treat a brief from a client with reverence. 'You couldn't touch it. You couldn't discuss it. You couldn't ask any questions... that might show a weakness or piss off the client – it was bizarre.' In those days he found it harder to crack briefs or come up with the right solutions because he didn't fully understand the problems. 'There's a lot of questions that I wanted to ask that I didn't ask,' he says. 'And of course the less you know, the less likely [it is] you're going to create a great idea. A great idea is not magic, it's not just out of the blue... for me the best ideas always come from the brief.'

Depending on the size of the problem, you can always add more areas into the brief if needed. Here are some criteria that can be used to beef out a brief by adding more details.

Background: Do you have any more information as to what has got you to this point?

Support: Is there any additional research or evidence that backs up your insight?

Tone: Is there a particular tone of voice or style that the idea needs to be in?

Feel/Think: What do you want people to feel or think after seeing this idea?

Now, what's your problem?

Introducing IRL

It's one thing to read about the theory of creativity, but it's another to put it into practice. That's why at the end of every chapter of this book is a section called IRL. For those who don't live on the internet, IRL stands for 'In Real Life' and it's the section that will help you bring to life some of the theory we've talked about with exercises and worksheets. We've just learnt all about what would go into a hypothetical brief to come up with a creative idea, and now it's time to actually do it.

It took me a long time to properly understand my personal learning style. I enjoy a bit of the theory, but I find that the lessons connect with me more intensely when I'm actually *doing*. That's why there are 13 IRL exercises throughout this book, so that *Killer Thinking* can be more than just a read that inspires you for a few hours and which you then put away. I want you to highlight, dog-ear, underline, scribble and use every page of this book like a textbook to help you achieve your true potential. Everyone has the ability for killer thinking, and my mission is to bring it out of you so a thousand killer ideas can blossom and help our world in every little way.

The IRL sections should be seriously fun. You can approach this book in any way that you want, but my advice is to read the entire thing from start to finish. That will give you a great overview, and hopefully inspire a few ideas along the way. Once you've done that, return to the first IRL exercise and complete them one by one. Each exercise should take from five to 30 minutes.

I always advise people to clear as much of their day as possible so they can really focus on themselves and their creativity. If you can, change up your environment so you have fewer distractions than in your usual work day and so it feels fresh, new and exciting (because it should be!). You can complete the exercises by yourself or with a trusted group. If you're doing it solo, just a pad and pens will do. If you're with friends or colleagues, grab some large white sheets of paper you can stick on a wall. Make sure everyone's had a chance to read through each of the steps beforehand. That will make the exercises a lot easier.

The IRL exercises are designed to spark conversation and help you see clearly how to apply killer thinking to whatever problem you're facing. You can do all of them in the order they're presented in here, or decide which ones are the most relevant for you.

To make the process even easier, I have created a bunch of customised worksheets and guides that you can download for free from timduggan.com.au/killerthinking along with the latest step-by-step instructions and more examples.

IRL

Step 1: Be Your Problem's Therapist

You need to understand your problem better than anyone else. To do that you:

1. must know the right questions to ask;
2. need a succinct bullseye of exactly who your target is; and
3. need a super clear creative brief.

Exercise 1: Questions Only

It's tempting to jump straight in to coming up with answers to any questions you might have, but one of the most illuminating exercises you can do to get to the centre of a problem is to do the exact opposite. Instead of coming up with answers, you should come up with as many questions – and only questions – as you can regarding your topic.

1. Write down the main problem that you're trying to answer.

Most of these exercises will be more impactful if you use a pen to write them out in a notebook or on a piece of paper. Start off by writing down the main problem you want to solve. If you haven't clarified your primary problem yet, then use this as an opportunity to explore the topic further and tease out the questions.

2. Write out as many questions as you can around your topic.

Set a timer for four minutes, and write down every question that you can think of related to the topic. Don't think about the answers, or how you're going to tackle it, just start writing as many different questions as you can think of.

Every creative idea is a solution for a problem, and by forcing yourself to think only in possibilities, you might begin exploring a wide variety of areas you hadn't considered before. Once you have a list of questions from this exercise, you can start thinking about how to answer them. Each answer will get you closer to really understanding each inch of the problem you're trying to solve.

Exercise 2: Your Ideal Persona

Narrowing your target market for your creative idea down to a single person is one of the best ways of making sure the end result will hit the mark. Here's how to do it.

1. Gather as much information about your audience as you can.

For some projects, this will come easily. You might have a trove of information about your target audience, like existing customer information, survey results or industry information. However, it's not 100 per cent necessary. In this step, pull together whatever you can find about the intended audience of your idea. If you don't have any, then just go straight to the next step and use your best educated guesses to help guide you.

2. Create an idealised profile of them.

Answer the following questions to create a profile of who you're aiming to reach and make an impact regarding a potential idea.

- What's their name?
- Where do they live?
- What job do they do?
- What's their home situation like?

- What do they do for fun?
- What media do they read/watch/listen to?
- What are their biggest frustrations?
- What are their biggest fears?
- What are their needs?

You can also flesh out the specific questions that relate to your particular problem. If you don't know all the answers, start improvising. You want to build up a picture of them so when you come up with ideas you can customise them for this exact person. Once you've answered some of the questions above, combine them into a single paragraph or page that sums up the ideal persona. You might even want to add a 'picture' you can find of the person to make it even more memorable for people. Remember that the aim is not to describe a real person, instead it should be an 'avatar' or 'persona' of members of the target market that will help you focus your ideas.

Exercise 3: The Creative Brief

The creative brief is your most important tool in coming up with killer ideas. Even if you don't think you need it, trust me on this one.

Write down the six core elements of a brief on one page. For a quick refresher of what we ran through earlier, the core components of a brief are:

- **Problem**
  What's the main problem you want to solve with a creative solution? Exercise 1 should have helped with clarifying this for you.

- **Audience**

  Who is your ideal target market? The persona you created in Exercise 2 can give a rounder picture of who are trying to speak to.

- **Objective**

  What do you want your idea to achieve? Try to keep this as clear, achievable, living and measurable as you can.

- **Insight**

  What's a core truth regarding someone's beliefs, behaviour or attitude? You will know a great insight when you hear it, as it will just help everything make more sense.

- **Essentials**

  What are the mandatories that your solution has to have? There is a lot of creativity in constraints, so make sure you list out everything that's on the list of non-negotiables here.

- **Actions**

  What do you actually want someone to do? Is this about selling more products, raising money or just making someone smile and feel better about themselves? You need to be clear on what Call to Action you're issuing.

If you can fit all these elements on a single page then you've got the best chance of other people giving your ideation their full attention. Many killer ideas have been lost in too many details, so try to keep your sentences short and to the point.

Fast Takeaways

1. Every creative idea is a response to a problem.
2. You need to know your problem inside out to understand every part of it.
3. Creativity involves switching between divergent thinking (generation of ideas) and convergent thinking (choosing the best ones).
4. To come up with killer ideas, you should spend one third of your time understanding the problem, one third on individual ideation and the last third on group creative sessions.
5. The ideal creative brief contains six main elements: problem, audience, objective, insight, essentials and actions.

Step 2:
Fit Your Own Mask First

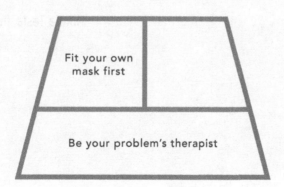

Fit your own
mask first

Be your problem's therapist

Be alone, that is the
secret of invention;
be alone, that is when
ideas are born.

Nikola Tesla, inventor

Fit Your Own Mask First

The more constraints you put on creativity, the more creative you must be. Take in-flight safety videos, for example. The detailed instructions given on every flight before take-off are a legal requirement of running an airline, and highly regulated in what they have to include: things like the location of the exits, how the seatbelts work or where the inflatable vests are.

Ever since screens were introduced on planes in the 1980s, safety videos have been a mainstay of all commercial flights. Most of them were pretty standard until airlines in the early 2000s realised they could differentiate their brands by making their safety videos unique.[19] Virgin America began animating their demonstration, Qatar Airlines filmed theirs at an FC Barcelona football match, British Airways used celebrities like Gordon Ramsay and Sir Ian McKellen, Air New Zealand recruited hobbits and Golden Girl Betty White, and Qantas retold the story of their 100-year history.

But despite all of the humour, flavour and gimmicks inserted into each of the scripts for the videos, the mandatory key points were always included in clever creative ways, and there was one line in every video that stood out for me. It was the moment when the oxygen masks fell from the ceiling and a parent and child were pictured seated next to each other. Most people's natural instinct would be to attach the oxygen to the children first before putting their own masks on, but the message was clear: 'Be sure to put your mask on before helping others.'

It's a counterintuitive message but it makes sense. You need to put your own mask on before you can reach out to help others. If not, you're putting yourself and others in danger instead of calmly prioritising your own health before you can look after other people.

The reason I always love this line when it appears in safety videos is because the message is so transferable to other aspects of life. It's been used in mental health, parenting and activism, and now I'm applying it to creativity. One of the biggest mistakes people make when trying to come up with ideas is to prematurely connect with others and try to do the work together. In other words, they fail to put on their own masks first. Group creative sessions are useful, but it's a lot more effective and necessary to do individual ideation first. Think of that as putting on your own mask before turning to others.

Creativity can be daunting, overwhelming and fun all at the same time, but you've got to give yourself permission to jump headfirst into your own thoughts and swim around in them before sharing those fragile ideas with other people.

Author, journalist and activist Sarah Wilson has written several bestselling books, including *First We Make the Beast Beautiful* and *This One Wild and Precious Life*. She half-jokingly summaries her creative process in one word: chaos. 'You've got to get messy,' she says. 'Over the years I've learnt that it's wallowing around in the messiness for quite some time that is necessary, and I allow myself that.'

By its very definition, allowing space for random thoughts to intersect in your mind as you play around with them can be confusing and hard at times. 'It is horrible,' says Sarah. 'It is painful, and deeply uncomfortable... but I just accept that is the way I do things, and that is the process I think of every creative: to eventually learn that your imperfect way is your way.'

When Sarah needs to be creative, she writes down ideas that come randomly to her on scrap pieces of paper and in the backs of notebooks. She spends a long time researching every part of a topic that she's thinking about. 'I don't like to start writing or creating a plan until I've absorbed everything and sat with it, and sat with it, and sat with it.'

Once the messiness starts to take some kind of shape in her mind, she carves out time in her diary to force herself to work on it, including creating self-imposed deadlines she just has to hit. 'I will feel sick if I don't meet it,' she says. 'I know myself well enough to know that things will become intolerable if it drags on.' For Sarah, creativity is a two-speed process, and both are needed to get her best work done. 'It's languid and loose and messy,' she says, 'and then it's hurry-the-fuck-up and get this done.'

English songwriter and musician Ed Sheeran has sold over 150 million records, and views creativity like a dirty tap. 'This is a weird analogy, but bear with me,' Ed told the Grammys Recording Academy in 2014.[20] 'Songwriting and gigs are like a dirty tap in an old house... when you switch on an old tap, it runs out muddy water for about a minute and then it starts flowing clean water.' Ed views the creativity involved in crafting lyrics and melodies in the same way. 'You'll switch on the tap and start writing songs and they'll be the worst songs you've ever written. They'll just be terrible, but once you've got them out you're unclogging the system... Once it starts flowing, you'll write good song after good song after good song. And once in a while, you'll write a bad song, and the important thing to remember is for that to not get you down, because you're still just unclogging the pipes.'

In order to come up with ideas by yourself, you need to open up the tap and let all the water flow out. So how to get your dirty tap flowing with clear water? After understanding every part of the problem, you've got to carve time out to think by yourself, without any interference from the opinions of others.

Making Time

At the end of every year Spotify pulls off one of their neatest tricks. They allow you to look back over the last 12 months of music you've listened to and use data visualisation to summarise your year in review. Spotify's annual Wrapped campaign shows you what you've actually spent your time absorbing, proving you're not the cool, edgy listener you think you are.

For the last three years, my annual Spotify Wrapped list has looked pretty boring. Every single year, there is one artist who sits at the top of my most played albums, and it's all because of a ritual.

If you want to be creative and shift your mind into a different gear from your usual frantic, jumpy thoughts, then it's important that you signify to yourself (and sometimes to others) that you're in a new mental mode.

For me, it's music. When I want to be creative, write, solve a problem, or spend some time deeply thinking about a problem, I do something that tells my brain it's time to switch modes and concentrate.

One of my favourite Australian music artists is Missy Higgins. The singer–songwriter has a uniquely Australian twang to her vocals and I've been listening to her telling stories through song for almost two decades, since she first debuted on Triple J's Unearthed when she was still at school.

Whenever I want to switch into a creative mood, I press play on Missy Higgins's compilation album *The Special Ones*. As soon as the opening guitar licks of the first track, 'Arrows', ring out and Missy drawls her opening lyrics, I kick straight into a different frame of mind. It's my own 'Pavlov's Dog' moment, where I've trained my creative juices to flow as soon as I hear the familiar chords. It doesn't matter if I'm in a crowded office, in my study or on a plane, it instantly transports me to my creative place (I'm even listening to the album right now as I type this).

My husband jokes he just hears the same songs playing over and over, but for me there's a meditative process to the repetitiveness. Every note is so well worn into the grooves of my memory, each song finishing and starting exactly as I expect it to, every sentence memorised, that when it plays it becomes background noise for my mind, transporting me to a Zen-like mode so I can properly think. That's the reason why, every single year, my most played artist on Spotify is always Missy Higgins, over and over.

Paul Graham, the co-founder of seminal venture capital firm Y Combinator, wrote an essay in 2009 in which he described two different ways of working: the Maker's Schedule and the Manager's Schedule. I didn't know it, but putting the same album on repeat was one of my first experiments with Maker Time, a concept first introduced to me by my friend the author Lorraine Murphy.

You can't be creative all the time: our brains just don't work like that. Maker Time is personal time for you to fit your own mask first, make things, break things, think and create. Manager Time is the mode to switch into to help you execute your killer ideas.

Manager Time

The Manager's Schedule is the traditional way business is run. Each day is divided up into, say, one-hour-long blocks that are typically booked up in advance with meetings, calls, brainstorms, or are occasionally blocked out to work on projects. Generally every hour or so the attention shifts from one task to the next. And repeat, every day. 'Most powerful people are on the manager's schedule,' wrote Paul in his essay. 'It's the schedule of command.'

Maker Time

Anyone who has to 'make' something, whether it's complete a big creative project, code software, tackle a big organisational problem, tends to think of time in at least units of half a day, sometimes full days. Anything shorter than that and it takes just as long to work up to hitting your full stride as it does to shut down. Makers need solid blocks of uninterrupted time to get things done.

Paul argued that since most powerful people operate on a Manager's Schedule at work out of sheer necessity, this attitude cascades through the organisation until every minute of every day is booked up in busy people's diaries, and everyone flits from one meeting to the next doing lots and lots of 'stuff'. It's basically a recipe for how to be uncreative. So what's the solution?

You've got to take back control of your own time management, and consciously decide if a block of time is going to be dedicated to being a Manager or a Maker. The ideal is to carve out entire days of your week, or at least half days, to either type of schedule and then stick to it. For example, if you want to be creative and solve problems or tackle bigger issues than what you can get done in the usual day-to-day, schedule an entire Maker Day a week. Book it out completely and fiercely protect it by allowing no meetings on that day if possible. I personally find that even just one meeting can blow your focus by forcing you to shift your thinking mode back into Manager mode so I try to completely block out my Maker Time. I devote mornings to thinking, writing, planning out big projects and strategising. This leaves afternoons for Manager Time, to respond to emails, schedule in meetings and generally power through my to-do list. It sounds simple, but this small shift in how I approach my work routine really helps me be creative when I need to be, and get everything done the rest of the time.

This is how to ensure Maker Time is firmly set onto your calendar.

Commit

Work calendars can get out of control very easily. Before you know it, every hour is jam-packed with meetings, often when just an email would do, and it becomes a fight to find time in your diary to stop and actually complete all the work you talk about. If you want to break that cycle, you have to actively push against it by committing a big chunk of your time to a Maker Schedule. If you can, block out an entire Maker Day at least once a fortnight. No meetings, few emails. Just you, a beautifully empty calendar, and a whopping big project that you're working on. Try to avoid Mondays and Fridays as they are generally weekend shoulder times and it's harder to get into a flow, and pick a day like Wednesday or Thursday as your Maker Day. Then stick to it and don't let anyone talk you out of it.

Communicate

Once you've chosen your day, or even half day if that works better, notify everyone who needs to know your plan. It's your diary and you should be able to control it, so tell everyone who matters that you plan for this time to be solo thinking time. In fact, you can even politely recommend they do the same thing! If everyone on your team schedules a Maker Day for the same time, there will be many fewer distracting emails trying to get your attention. Update your email auto-responder to let people know you'll get back to them later. If you're going to fit your own mask first, you need to ensure others know that's what you're doing.

Connect

Do something during your Maker Time that you connect only with creative work – a ritual that sets it apart from your usual time, like lighting a candle, putting on an essential-oil diffuser, or playing a particular album or soundtrack that you reserve just for this time.

Smell is an under-utilised sense, and it's very easy to create an association between a particular smell and being creative. When I want to get into the zone I love putting a diffuser on with local native essential oils, especially something punchy like eucalyptus. One whiff of that, and I flick into creative mode.

Change

The best way to signify the mental shift between Manager and Maker times is to physically change your environment. If you're working from home, try sitting in a new spot. If you're in the office, close the door to a meeting room or find a quiet space somewhere you won't be disturbed. You need to signify to your mind, and to others, that this is a different headspace where you're going to think in a different way. If you really can't move anywhere new, then even a simple act like putting headphones in to listen to soft music (Missy Higgins, anyone?) can be enough to signify change. When I'm at home I have a simple trick I use to mentally shift my mind between Maker and Manager times. When I'm in Manager Time, I tend to sit at my desk in my home library. When I switch to Maker Time, I take my laptop computer and snuggle up on the couch or on my bed. It's a simple change that takes a minute to execute, but it tells my brain (and my husband) which mode I'm in.

There are different variations you can adapt to suit your circumstances. Theatre director and playwright Declan Greene calls his Manager Time 'tasks' and his Maker Time 'dreaming', dividing the former into 15-minute blocks of tasks, and for the latter allowing longer unstructured periods of time to think deeply about his work. Declan was diagnosed with ADHD a few years ago, and says that having a better understanding of how his brain works has been extremely helpful to his life. 'When I'm tackling any creative project, I now write up a timeline and workflow,' he says. His Manager Time (or 'tasks') is for playwriting and research, and involves compiling notes, structure documents and scene breakdowns, 'and a lot of list-making'. His Maker Time (or 'dreaming', in his words) is for writing dialogue, inventing characters and crafting the plot. 'Early on I was concerned that this approach was antithetical to a creative process, which we often expect should be free and open and guided by intangible things like inspiration,' says Declan. 'But it's really helped me understand that parameters can be so important for the creation of inspiration.'

Everyone has a different ritual they perform to get creative. Joel Connolly is the creative director at Blackbird, Australia's largest venture capitalist firm, which has invested in many of the country's most successful tech companies, including Canva, SafetyCulture and Culture Amp. Joel has a ritual when he needs to signal to his brain that it's time to get creative: he stands up. He has a whiteboard hanging on a wall of his office that he uses to flesh out his thoughts. 'I'll get out of my chair and I'll move around a bunch,' he says. 'I've found that, over time, that's the thing that works best for me.'

Author and entrepreneur Lisa Messenger needs to draw circles to connect her ideas visually. 'There is not a day that goes by where I don't draw a mind map!' she says. 'I always have an A4 notepad next to me and I'm always using it to visualise where I think I'm going, what I could do with something and what it looks like.'

Designer and artist Evi O says that beats help her kick into the right mode. 'Playing electronic, techno and lady rap music gets me into a state of productivity.'

Abigail Forsyth, the co-founder of KeepCup, whips out stationery. 'I'll get out the tracing paper... and draw things out,' she says of her creative ritual. 'My husband now knows what's about to happen and he's learnt to just let me do it. It might be an idea that never eventuates, but I have to follow the process through to the other side.'

Perhaps the most extreme example of a creative ritual is that of author Jonathan Franzen. To write his bestselling books like *Freedom*, he needs to clear all distractions. The *Guardian* describes his writing studio as a 'monastic cell': 'His computer has had its card removed, so he cannot be tempted by computer games,' they wrote. 'The ethernet port has been physically sealed, so he cannot connect to the internet.' Once he's in his 'cell', Franzen places earplugs in both ears then covers them with noise-cancelling headphones that play white noise at a very low frequency.[21] When he wrote *The Corrections*, he even wore a blindfold as he touch-typed. That's obviously an intense form of disconnecting, but everyone's routine for coming up with ideas independently is different, and you need to find the one that works best for you.

Be the Change

Jay Coen Gilbert started his professional life in a pretty traditional way. After graduating from Stanford University in California he followed a well-worn path for many alumni into management consultancy, getting a graduate job with McKinsey. It didn't take long for him to discover he didn't aspire to climb the corporate ladder; Jay wanted to do something more fun and aligned with his interests, and he'd often throw around random business ideas with one of his best friends.

After a year or so of going back and forth on different ideas together, they landed on one that felt a bit different and spent a night at a jazz club in Philadelphia writing their ideas down on napkins and coasters. 'By the end of that weekend,' recalls Jay, 'I had been infected with a virus that said, "That would be a really fun thing to do. And I get to do that with my best friend."'

Jay and his friends Seth Berger and Tom Austin were keen basketball fans who could sense an ascendant moment in the United States in which basketball, hip hop and the internet were about to collide. Their idea was to create a clothing brand built on the culture of basketball. They began by selling trash-talking T-shirts aimed squarely at players with slogans like *Here's $5. Go buy a game*, and *I'm sorry. I thought you could play*. Within their first year their new company, AND1, had revenue of US$1.7 million, then grew rapidly alongside the cultural currency of basketball into a very successful business selling shoes and clothes to a close-knit community of basketball lovers. 'I play basketball,' jokes Jay, 'but poorly and it's not my identity. The people who we were building this for, and the other co-founders, you could cut them open and they would bleed orange like the colour of a basketball... There's something about the idea of creating a community for people who share an incredible passion for something that was incredibly attractive to me.' By the time they sold the company, 12 years later, AND1 had global revenue of US$250 million and was the number-two basketball shoe seller in the United States after Nike.

That all sounds pretty straightforward, right? Like most things in life, behind the scenes it was anything but. AND1 co-founder Tom Austin can recall a timeline of failures that almost wiped out the company half a dozen times.[22] From initial customers not paying for orders to a similar-sounding skateboard company trying to sue them out of existence, to 24,000 shoes being returned for defects and various product launch failures that threatened the company's future, their road to success – like everyone's – was paved with potholes they never saw coming.

Jay left AND1 when it was sold in 2005 and took a year off full-time working. He realised he needed time unattached to 'what's next', instead of jumping straight into the next opportunity. He travelled with his young family around Australia, New Zealand and Costa Rica, using the time to think deeply about what he wanted to do next. 'The most important thing that happened over those 12 months was that I had enough space, and a completely different perspective on life, to be able to make an affirmative decision on exactly what I wanted to do,' says Jay. 'Ideas evolve when you have a little bit more distance.'

For his first business, Jay had listened to the ball players on the courts telling him what they wanted in their products. For his next idea he also listened, this time to entrepreneurs. One idea that had been floating around his head was how he could build a business that was kinder and had potential for a bigger impact. He was intrigued by Newman's Own, a company started by the actor Paul Newman, and best known for tasty salad dressings, which donated 100 per cent of its profits to charities that support education. The company has been so wildly successful that it's donated over US$550 million to charity since 1982. 'I was quite inspired by that in the purity of an evergreen engine for charitable giving to do good in the world,' says Jay. He spent time thinking about 'business for good', doing research and studying other successful companies like Ben & Jerry's, Patagonia, Stonyfield Farm and Tom's of Maine. As he looked, he realised there were dozens of companies that donated 100 per cent of their profits to for-purpose charities and other places that did good.

Jay's original idea was to create a logo for all these businesses that were donating 100 per cent of their profits to charity to add to their products so consumers could easily recognise them. It was a simple idea, and he shared it with other entrepreneurs. They liked it, but gave him feedback that donating money to good causes – whether 10 per cent or 100 per cent – is just one way a business can have a positive impact; how they actually ran the company was more important.

It wasn't something Jay had properly registered until then. 'Part of listening is connecting dots and then putting something out there and then listening, again, for the response,' says Jay. 'Being a really good listener may get you part of the way, but then you also have to be able to connect some dots or see around the corner in a way that one plus one plus one equals five, not three.'

The realisation that a business's impact could be measured and tracked using various criteria was a revelation for Jay. 'It basically widened the aperture of my lens to see that charitable giving was not the only material way to create a positive impact with a company; it certainly wasn't the most impactful way.' That gradually led Jay and his partners to the idea of building a set of standards businesses can adhere to that would look holistically at how the business operates.

The next two or three years involved a lot of listening to hundreds of entrepreneurs, early-stage investors, academics and thought leaders, before Jay and his co-founders Bart Houlahan and Andrew Kassoy launched B Lab in 2006, the social enterprise behind the B Corp system, in which companies can put themselves through a series of vigorous tests to receive official certification as a B Corp. Over 120,000 companies around the world are now using the B Impact Assessment as an impact management tool, and 4,000 have certified as B Corps that balance purpose and profit, with that number growing every day. B Corps are a breakthrough idea, showing companies and leaders a framework in which they can create value not just for shareholders, but also the environment, the local community and their employees.

Jay continues to think about how he can make even more of a difference, and recently worked with B Lab to launch another venture to refine his thinking and amplify their impact. If the B Corp movement is building change from the ground up, one company at a time, Imperative 21 is designed to come at it the other way: working to build a broader coalition of organisations who all share a vision. It's a business-led network with an aim to reset our economic system to create shared wellbeing on a healthy planet and represents more than 134,000 businesses across 80 countries, 25 million employees and $11 trillion in combined revenue. 'You might get 4,000 or 10,000 companies around the world that are strong enough to swim against the current,' Jay says of the current B Corp movement, 'but we need to do more than that. We need to shift the current. And you can think of the current as culture, and structures, and systems, and incentives that are all working at cross purposes with "business for good".'

Throughout Jay's career, from AND1 to B Corp to Imperative 21, one common thread is the importance of taking time out to connect dots and opportunities. Not everyone has the luxury to take a year off to do it, but anyone can learn the lesson that removing yourself from the everyday can pay off in massive ways.

Make Connections

Once you've carved out some personal time to be creative, it's time to turn on the dirty tap and see what comes out. Some people get overwhelmed by a blank page, but there are simple techniques you can do at this stage to get the water running clear.

Ideas can easily escape your grip, but one of the most straightforward ways to generate them is to ask what happens when you combine two or more concepts together. 'Creativity is just connecting things,' Steve Jobs told *WIRED* magazine in 1996.[23] 'When you ask creative people how they did something, they feel a little guilty because they didn't really do it, they just saw something. It seemed obvious to them after a while. That's because they were able to connect experiences they've had and synthesise new things. And the reason they were able to do that was that they've had more experiences or they have thought more about their experiences than other people.'

Apple became one of the world's most valuable companies by selling products that combine two ideas: the iPhone (a phone and a computer), Apple Watch (a watch and a computer), iPad (a tablet and a computer), and one day maybe even an iCar (one of Jobs's last big ideas before he died in 2011 was to combine modern car design with a drivable computer).[24] Sometimes, creativity is just connecting things.

In entrepreneurship, there's even a common way of pitching ideas to venture capitalists for funding that quickly fills them in on what you do by combining two known concepts together:

- The Airbnb of parking
- The Uber of flowers
- The Spotify of education

As clichéd as they are, these shortcuts work because everyone knows about the concepts of parking, flowers and education as well as the businesses Airbnb, Uber and Spotify. Combining them is an easy way of explaining a bigger idea without having to use many words.

Netflix is now one of the most iconic entertainment companies in the world, but it wasn't always that way. In fact, when the co-founders tried to come up with a name for their new company they had a lot of trouble. Marc Randolph, Netflix's co-founder, explained what happened.[25] They got everyone into a conference room and made two columns on a whiteboard. In one column, they wrote down every possible word they could think of that brought to mind the internet. Words like web and net and 'e-'anything. In the other column they added words that conjured up video or rental. They then started drawing lines to connect these random words together.

They created a lot of random names: Cinema Centre, Web Flix, Net Flicks and Net Flix. 'Net Flix was far and away no one's favourite,' said Marc. 'Back in the '60s and '70s the nickname for porno used to be… "skin flicks". Everyone was going, "We can't call it flicks and that x is even worse!"' They tried lots of other options, but after failing to get the domain name or trademark for anything else, they had to make a decision. They half-heartedly decided to go with the name that combined two things together. 'Netflix was a little porn-y, but it was the best that we could do!' Marc laughs now.

The business world can learn a lot about generating and refining ideas from more traditional creatives like authors, musicians and comedians. Take Jerry Seinfeld: his creativity turned a show about nothing into something extremely valuable. His eponymous show, created with Larry David, is the most successful television comedy series in history, running for nine seasons and named the best sitcom ever by *60 Minutes* and *Vanity Fair* in 2012, and offering the greatest television episode of all time, as named by *TV Guide* in

2009 (for season four's episode 'The Contest', by the way). On top of being critically acclaimed and loved by millions, *Seinfeld* was worth US$500 million to Netflix, which secured the exclusive streaming rights to all 180 episodes for five years from 2021.[26]

In December 2020, Jerry sat down with author Tim Ferriss on his podcast to explain his creative process.[27] 'My writing sessions used to be very arduous, very painful, like pushing against the wind in soft, muddy ground with a wheelbarrow full of bricks,' he said. 'And I did it. I had to do it because… you either learn to do that or you will die in the ecosystem. I learnt that really fast and really young, and that saved my life and made my career.'

Jerry has multiple tricks to keep his creativity on track. The first is that he keeps a small notebook of observations with him, and is constantly adding to it. 'Just really, really random things,' he says, like one-liners he hears in everyday conversations that intrigue him.

The second is that he schedules in a writing session with a very specific start and end time. 'Don't just sit down with an open-ended, "I'm going to work on this problem." That's a ridiculous torture to put on a human being's head,' he says. 'It's like you're going to hire a trainer to get in shape, and he comes over, and you go, "How long is the session?" And he goes, "It's open-ended." Forget it. I'm not doing it. It's over right there. You've got to control what your brain can take.'

His final piece of advice is that even he, someone who has been regarded as one of the greatest comedy writers in history, still doesn't believe his own hype. When asked how he would teach creativity to someone, Jerry said: 'I would teach them to learn to accept your mediocrity. No one's really that great. You know who's great? The people that just put tremendous amount of hours into it. It's a game of tonnage.'

After you've defined the problem you're trying to solve, start by looking at any solutions that exist for it already and see if there's a way of combining elements to create something new. Brand-new ideas are very rare. Most new ideas are remixes of existing ones, with some elements dialled up or down to make them better. Let the dirty water flow out before the clean water can come, so don't worry if you think your first ideas aren't great. The more water you get flowing, the better your ideas will be.

IRL

Step 2: Fit Your Own Mask First

Don't dive straight into creative ideation with a group until you've spent time thinking about it by yourself. Consciously plan to switch into Maker mode and let your imagination go wild. Just the thought of this can scare some people, and leave others scratching their heads at where to start, so here's how to go about it.

Exercise 4: Maker/Manager Calendar

If you want to be creative and productive, you need to schedule in both Maker and Manager time, but when is the best time? This will be different for everybody, and depends on your schedule, energy levels and other commitments. To make your own Maker/Manager Calendar, just follow these steps.

1. Draw up a calendar of the last seven days.

Create a simple table that has each day of the week on it, and then some key time periods, like 'before work', 'morning', 'afternoon' and 'after work'. You can adapt these time periods if you want to get even more granular with this exercise. The table should look like this:

	Monday	Tuesday	Wednesday	Thursday	Friday	Saturday	Sunday
Early morning							
Morning							
Afternoon							
Evening							

You can also download a free template of this calendar from timduggan.com.au/killerthinking to help you complete this exercise.

2. Rate your energy levels during each period from 1 to 10.

You can either do this in retrospect, thinking back to how you've felt over the last seven days, or fill this out from today onwards for the next week. Record how you're feeling during each chunk of time, with 1 representing extremely low energy levels, and 10 signifying that you're basically jumping around the room. Most of us aren't consciously aware of our energy levels all the time, so this exercise will force you to think about how you're feeling. It can help to set a regular timer on your phone to check in every few hours on how you're feeling.

3. Add up each of the rows.

Once you've filled in your energy levels for different times of the day, add up the rows to get a total. It should like something like this:

	Monday	Tuesday	Wednesday	Thursday	Friday	Saturday	Sunday	
Early morning	6	5	7	6	4	3	3	34
Morning	8	6	9	8	6	4	3	44
Afternoon	5	5	8	6	3	6	7	40
Evening	7	4	5	6	2	5	5	34

The number at the right-hand side is your energy level during that time of day, added up over a total seven-day period. You can adapt this as much as you'd like, taking into account which days of the week you like to work and adding more details of your day, with additional headings like 'after exercise' or 'late night'. The cumulative number should give you an indication of when your energy levels are at the highest and lowest throughout the day. If I plotted the totals on a line graph, the above table is telling me that my energy levels are highest in the morning, drop a bit in the afternoon and are at their lowest during the early morning and evening time. That feels about right, given how I like to plan out my day.

4. Schedule Maker Time when your energy levels are highest.

You can then schedule in your Maker and Manager times to take advantage of your varying energy levels. Most people need higher energy levels when it's time to be creative, so look at the times when your energy is the highest, and begin scheduling in large chunks of Maker Time on those days and times. Manager Time is for responding to emails and other more 'manual'-type tasks, which can be done at any time, regardless of energy levels. I prefer Maker Time when my energy is high, and Manager Time during the lower period, but once you're aware of it you can create your own personal Maker and Manager Calendar by observing your energy on different days and times.

Exercise 5: Your Creative Ritual

When it's time to get thinking, you need a signal to yourself, and everyone around you, that you need some space to connect with your creative side. So, how do you do that?

1. Pick a sense.

We have five senses, yet we rarely think about their key roles in helping us switch between the moods that we're in. Choose the sense that best speaks to you, or if you can't settle on just one, you can always pick more.

Smell: Is there a fragrance you can associate with creativity?

Hearing: What's a soundtrack that signals the mood change?

Taste: Is there a food or snack you can eat or drink to help you think up ideas?

Sight: What view gets your creative juices flowing?

Touch: Is there a tactile object you can play with?

2. Choose a ritual you can easily stick to.

Once you've settled on your favourite sense, or two, decide on something easy you can do to begin the mental association between smelling, hearing or seeing this ritual, and coming up with lots of ideas. Here are some suggestions.

Smell
- Lighting a candle
- Burning essential oils or incense
- Spraying cleaning products
- Hanging an air-freshener

Hearing
- Putting on a familiar music soundtrack or playlist
- Listening to bird calls
- Using noise-cancelling headphones to block out sound
- The gentle whirr of a fan

Taste
- Chewing on a mint or gum
- Eating snacks with strong memories attached to them
- Flavoured water or drinks
- Drinking tea or coffee

Sight
- Sitting in the same spot each time
- An expansive view of the landscape
- Staring at artwork on the wall
- Flicking through a magazine for inspiration

Touch

- Playing around with a stress ball or small object
- Holding whiteboard markers and writing on the wall
- Touching nature on an outdoor walk
- Sitting in your favourite comfy chair

3. Set up your ritual every time you want to think.

The final step is to forge the connection between your ritual and your creative time. If you perform your ritual like a ceremony every time you prepare to work creatively, before long just the act of setting up for the ritual (like preparing a cup of tea) will signal to your mind that it's time to think. All I now need is one line of Missy Higgins singing and I switch directly into Maker Time.

Exercise 6: The Dirty Tap

There is nothing more frustrating than sitting in front of an empty page when your mind keeps drawing blanks. When that happens, there's a couple of very simple techniques to get some ideas going and to turn on the dirty tap until it's all flowing out of you.

1. Set a goal.

It doesn't need to be a momentous objective, but a solid way of getting your ideas going is to give yourself a few small goals at the start. It could be:

- Come up with ten ideas
- Write a full page of words
- Think for the next 20 minutes
- Combine 30 names

Starting with a number gives you something to aim towards, as well as a sense of achievement when you reach it. Remember you need to keep going and come up with lots of ideas before you get to the good ones.

2. Set some boundaries.
Blank pages are often caused by having too many options. Choose what boundaries you wish to create for yourself, and you'll be thinking of ways around them in no time. Things like:

- the idea can only be one syllable long;
- the name needs to use alliteration;
- you can only use items already in the room; or
- any other constraint you can think of.

Our minds love to work within rules, and bend our ways around them. Giving yourself boundaries, even if artificial, will help us think laterally.

3. Set a timer.
The sure-fire way to generate ideas is to give yourself a deadline. Set a timer on your phone for ten minutes, and then force yourself to come up with something. You can combine this idea-generating exercise with the ones above to really add some pressure, but there's something about deadlines that makes our mind focus on just the task at hand.

These are some simple exercises designed to get you generating ideas. Try not to edit and refine your ideas as there will be plenty of time to do that later: for now, your job is just to turn on that dirty tap and let as much water as possible flow right on out.

Fast Takeaways

1. You have to come up with your own ideas before group thinking to let real diversity of imagination shine through.

2. Creativity is like a dirty tap. At the start the water is going to be a bit murky, but you need to keep going and generate lots of thoughts before the clear water (i.e. good ideas) can come out.

3. There are two types of working: Maker Time, when you can think freely about projects; and Manager Time, when you get things done.

4. Most workplaces prioritise Manager Time out of necessity, so you need to consciously schedule Maker Time by committing to it, communicating the commitment to everyone, connecting a ritual with it and changing your environment.

5. A lot of creativity is just connecting two things that already exist in a new way.

Step 3:
'Plus' Each Other's Ideas

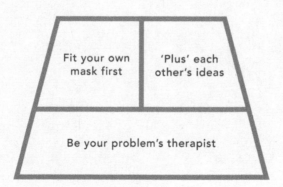

Fit your own mask first

'Plus' each other's ideas

Be your problem's therapist

None of us is as smart
as all of us.

Ken Blanchard, author

'Plus' Each Other's Ideas

Alinea is one of the most awarded and respected restaurants in the US. With three Michelin stars, and having often been ranked as one of the top 50 restaurants in the world for over a decade,[28] the restaurant serves food that is unbelievably tricky molecular gastronomy, food that has you shaking your head in disbelief as you dine. 'Whether you are seated at the kitchen table, gallery or salon, dining here is part theatre and pure pleasure,' reads the official Michelin guide.[29] 'Meals take advantage of every sense, so expect scented vapours, tricks, and tableside preparations.' Some of the experimental food served to diners in Chicago includes liquified caramel popcorn, a sheet of raspberry transparency and a dish involving a balloon made out of mozzarella.

When visual effects artist and blogger Allen Hemberger dined there with his wife Sarah, he was blown away by the sheer levels of creativity coming out of the kitchen of visionary chef Grant Achatz and his team. 'I didn't really think of it as anything particularly different from anything else I'd ever eaten before until I got there,' he said.[30] 'Then I was like, what is this?!... Oh my gosh, I'd never seen anything like this. How are they doing this? How does this work?'

Sarah gave Allen a copy of Alinea's cookbook for Christmas and they marvelled over the daunting instructions on how to construct 107 of the most iconic dishes. The book was full of equipment Allen had never heard of, and ingredients straight out of a chemistry textbook, but one day he tried making the shortest recipe. It was for 'dry caramel salt' and his first attempt was a fail. He tried again, and couldn't do it. Finally, on his third attempt, he recreated the dish and was extremely chuffed with the result. Allen was a writer and amateur photographer so he set up a home studio to capture the 'salt' in all its sweet, granulated glory and posted a blog about his attempts. He soon felt compelled to attempt another dish, and then another, trying to recreate and photograph each of the recipes inside the complicated cookbook. 'Each dish was its own little challenge,' he said.

Some of the recipes required expensive technical equipment, so he built his own precisely controllable heating chamber to warm chocolate to exactly 94 degrees Fahrenheit, just under its melting point, made out of a foam cooler, a halogen work light and a temperature controller.[31] He played with liquid nitrogen and paint spray guns, and took up machinery classes to learn how to make some of the custom dish-wear that the food was presented in. He even had to figure out how to import super-fresh fish from the Tsukiji fish market in Japan just to try to complete one of the dishes in the book. The project became an obsession, and the untrained chef spent the next five years trying to perfect all of the 107 complex recipes by himself.

He documented every misstep and success along the way, working with Sarah to take 13,000 photos of his experiments. Their apartment resembled a laboratory, and Allen relished the chance to explore creative expression through molecular gastronomy, figuring most of it out himself late at night, failed experiment after failed experiment. He didn't originally set out to make every recipe in the book. 'I just kind of kept going,' he's said. 'I don't ever remember making the decision, "I'm going to make everything." It was more that I never made the decision to stop.'

Allen put his own mask on first, exploring his creativity as far as he could on his own. He conquered the 'English peas' made from tofu, ham and a pillow of lavender air. He perfected the pork with grapefruit, sage and honeycomb. He even recreated the bubble gum, long pepper and hibiscus creme fraiche. 'It was a little bit addictive,' he said. 'Every time I'd finish one dish I would just be excited to do the next one.'

But about halfway through the project, he hit a wall. There was one particular recipe he couldn't master. It didn't matter how many times he tried it, or how closely he followed the printed words on the page, the final dish failed him over and over again. It was an extremely difficult recipe involving two spiral gels ('A ridiculous dish,' said Allen), and every time he attempted to make it, the gels would crack or flop over and collapse. Allen blamed himself for the failure. Of course a home chef couldn't recreate it perfectly, he told himself, it was all his fault. Allen couldn't get the recipe to work, so he did something he hadn't done before and 'cheated' by changing the recipe and adding more gelatine than was written down. His modification made a firmer gel and he was finally able to complete the dish. It tasted wonderful, but he couldn't shake the thought that he had somehow cheated.

As he was working his way through the recipes, Allen would occasionally email Grant Achatz updates and often received short, brusque responses back. Frustrated by the spiral, Allen emailed asking if he had any advice on how to do it right. Grant responded with a one-line email: *Can you fly to Chicago and I will give you a demo?*

Allen jumped on a plane to head to the restaurant, half expecting the professional chef to quickly show him how to roll the gelatine out properly. When he arrived at the back-lane workers' entrance, a few dozen chefs were crammed inside preparing the day's meals, all bustling action in one of the most sought-after kitchens in the world. The head chef pulled out some gelatine papers and asked Allen to show him exactly what he did wrong, and they tried to recreate the problem together.

As soon as the gelatine was set, Grant tried to roll them together in the same way as his own instructions in the book. On his first go, it cracked. He tried again, and the same thing happened. Grant casually told Allen that the recipe must be wrong, and to fix it he just needed to add more gelatine. It was exactly the same conclusion the home chef had come to all by himself. 'I was right,' explained Allen later. 'It was kind of an amazing moment... up to that point, when things went wrong it was because I had messed up... I sort of learnt how to trust myself.' Allen spent the rest of the afternoon in the Alinea kitchen, observing Grant work his magic and even helping the professional chefs plate up the final dishes for customers.

Allen returned to San Francisco, and spent the next few years with Sarah turning their recipe tests into a book, *The Alinea Project*. A Kickstarter campaign raised US$42,000 to publish it, and the first copy of the book was sent off to Alinea's co-owners Grant Achatz and Nick Kokonas. 'This would probably be a good place for this story to end, but it doesn't,' said Allen when he retold his adventures on stage at Chicago Ideas Week. Within a day of receiving the book, Grant and Nick called up Allen and Sarah. 'This is crazy,' they said, 'and we really like working with crazy people.'

A few years earlier Grant and Nick had opened up The Aviary, a unique cocktail bar in Chicago where they could apply the techniques of their kitchens to cocktails. Think drinks like 'In the Rocks', a twisted version of an Old Fashioned encased in an ice egg that you shatter with a tiny slingshot device, or a liquid nitrogen shot of ginger, lime juice, sugar and water that's been dusted around the glass like snow.[32] They wanted to somehow document the creativity of The Aviary, but had no idea where to begin.

Then they received Allen and Sarah's book in the mail. 'It immediately clicked to me,' said Nick.[33] 'Here are people who understand what it is that we're trying to do at The Aviary.' As they flipped through the book, they saw they had finally discovered other creatives to help bring to life their big vision without compromise. 'We didn't know anyone nutty enough to do this with us in a way that also felt new and different.' They asked Sarah and Allen to come join them full-time in Chicago. Allen and Sarah both quit their jobs and moved three-quarters of the way across the country to begin an unlikely creative collaboration, with each of the individuals bringing fresh ideas to build on top of each other.

Of course, it didn't start off exactly that way. During one of their first meetings together, they all stared at one another. 'We asked them, "What do you guys want this book to be?"' explained Allen.[34] 'They both shrugged and said, "We don't know; what do *you* want it to be?" It was not a question we were prepared to answer; we simply wanted to work with the incredibly talented staff to create something beautiful.'

They soon leant into making and photographing the book, sharing ideas on how to best capture the essence of The Aviary and produce the world's most beautiful cocktail book. The result took two years to make and was just as impressive an achievement, followed later by *ZERO: A New Approach to Non-Alcoholic Drinks*, with over 250 pages of stunning photography and illustrations of unique drink combinations – and not one reference to 'mocktails'.

Since 2016, Sarah and Allen have settled into their roles as the Directors of Media and Publishing at The Alinea Group, leading the art direction, design and illustration across all the group's restaurants and cookbooks. The owners and creatives constantly push each other to produce exceptional work. For Sarah and Allen, it's been a fruitful, and unexpected, pivot that demonstrates the power of coming together with other people and building on top of each other's ideas to help make them even better.

Plussing It

There are few people in history who have traded in ideas as much as Walt Disney, the American entrepreneur, animator, writer, voice actor and film producer. Although he has a complicated personal history that doesn't stand up to scrutiny today,[35] his influence on the world of creativity is undeniable. He instilled a culture of striving for that little bit extra that still runs through the company.

One concept he coined and encouraged in all of his employees is 'plussing'. It was his way of turning a good idea into a great one, by taking something people had created and figured out how to 'plus' it to give it that extra edge.

Walt used 'plussing' as a verb. In a 1956 interview talking about the thinking behind Disneyland, he described the benefit of continually refining ideas until they got better: 'I wanted something live, something that could grow, something I could keep plussing with ideas, you see? The park is that,' said Walt.[36] 'Not only can I add things, but even the trees will keep growing; the thing will get more beautiful every year.'

When Disney was creating his animated feature *Bambi* in the 1940s, he wanted the animals to look as realistic as possible, not just like cartoons. He plussed it by getting experts on anatomy to teach the animators, and even created a small zoo in the studio complete with rabbits, ducks, owls and even a pair of fawns so the artists could copy their movements directly.[37]

The idea of 'plussing' is inherent in really great ideas. It's what helps make them even more impactful, one of the key components of KILLER, and able to reach the most people in the deepest possible way. Keep in mind that impactful doesn't mean it needs to be the largest or the biggest. Impactful, here, is about how lasting your effect can be on people. You might only want to reach dozens of people, but if you can have a meaningful impact on them, then what you're doing is well on its way to being a truly killer idea.

After you've understood the problem, and made some time to come up with your own ideas, take the opportunity to get together with other people to start sharing those ideas and connecting them with others. See if you can collectively turn an idea into something better with group ideation.

This is the part where most people jump straight into a technique that's spread throughout every workplace in the world for more than 50 years: brainstorms. It's easy to understand why – there are in fact four reasons brainstorms have become the dominant form of creativity in the workplace.

Little preparation: You don't have to think about it before you sit down in a room together (which is surely half the problem, right?).

Quick: You can sit down with a group and come up with at least some basic ideas in just a few minutes. I mean, they might not be any good, but at least they're a start.

Easy: There's nothing complicated about it. Even my 98-year-old nonna would know what a brainstorm is. It's become the universal way of generating and collecting ideas.

Time limit: Put a half-hour brainstorm into a diary, and if you don't have something good within the first 15 minutes, you're damn sure you will come up with *something* in the last 15.

These are the main reasons that brainstorms have, well, stormed into most workplaces around the world. But they still suck. The idea for brainstorming came from advertising executive Alex Osborn, one of the founders of creative agency BBDO (the O in the name stands for Osborn). In 1942 he published a book, *How To 'Think Up'*, in which he argued that creativity was a muscle anyone could develop and proposed the concept of brainstorming (which he originally called 'thinking up').[38] The key to success of group creative sessions, he said, was to drop all judgement at the door and let all ideas, no matter how good or bad, bubble up to the surface. 'The crazier the idea, the better,' he wrote; 'it's easier to tone down than to think up.'

Brainstorms took hold and became the dominant way for groups to exercise creativity together. But we need to talk about the elephant in the room at every creative brainstorm. Actually, it's not really an elephant, it's a HIPPO.

Now, I don't mean the impressively large animals you might find in Africa. When we're talking about creativity at work, a HIPPO refers to something that can kill an idea before it has the chance to evolve into a killer idea. HIPPO stands for: HIghest Paid Person's Opinion.

We're all familiar with HIPPOs – heck, if I'm honest, I've even been one. Often the most senior person in a room has to be deferred to when an idea is suggested. Sometimes the HIPPO doesn't even need to be in the room for everyone to self-censor according to what they think this person would or wouldn't like. Thankfully, there are solutions on how to navigate around HIPPOs and their purveyors so everyone gets a chance to be heard equally when generating ideas.

There's an entire stream of research that focuses on the flaws of the usual format of creative brainstorming, and most of them tend to focus on the psychology of groupthink. If you get a collective of people together, there are always going to be intricate interpersonal dynamics that underpin it all. Some people might be shy or nervous about communicating their ideas; others will dominate and lead the group down the path they want to take.

There's also another big problem with the brainstorm that was devised 80 years ago: workplaces have changed. The 1940s style of collaboration involved getting all workers together in a physical space, and it was a working style that held up well until it didn't.

The modern workplace experimented with telephone conferencing from the 1990s onwards, then flirted with video calls and Skype in the early 2010s. And then Covid-19 spread, upending every workplace in the world basically overnight, and forcing society to adapt more quickly than it would have without a pandemic. Instead of gathering around a boardroom table to come up with ideas collectively, we would all dial into Zoom from our respective homes and try to abide by the same rules as used for in-person sessions.

Brainstorms on video conferences are something else: the awkward silences, unstable connections, one person dominating, others checking out. They usually devolve into two-person conversations with various bystanders politely listening in.

Malcolm Gladwell, the author and podcast host, agrees with his. He started an audio company, Pushkin Industries, with the former CEO of the Slate Group, Jacob Weisberg, in 2018 that grew to employ more than 40 staff in its first two years. Their company had one year of working together in an office, and then another year of working virtually as Covid-19 forced most companies to work from home for most of 2020. The two years of different working cultures gave Malcolm a rare insight. 'There are certain things we do that we've realised have become really hard remotely,' Malcolm told a webcast in early 2021. 'If you're trying to brainstorm on some complicated project and you need seven people in a room, Zoom just does not work. It's OK, it's not the same thing.' Malcom is right. Video conferencing was not designed for deep thinking or group work.

'I don't like brainstorming,' says Joel Connolly from Blackbird, 'but I do love coming into a room with people and going, "Here's all my ideas. What do you have to add to it?" Just the act of speaking about it, you find things go back and forth and people challenge me on it. That leads to creativity, instead of going into a room full of people and trying to come up with something from nothing.'

There has to be a better way, right?

There are few things that were introduced almost a hundred years ago that we are still doing today, and creative brainstorming is one of them. It's hardly changed in that time and often has the unintended effect of stifling creativity. The good news is that after studying countless research papers and conducting creative experiments in companies of all different sizes, I know there is a better way to do creative ideation and come up with killer ideas. And it still ticks off each of the four main reasons brainstorms have become so popular: little preparation, quick, easy and can be done within a time limit.

Let's get one thing clear right here: coming up with ideas should be fun. We are playing – tickling the creative parts of our minds – and if it's not fun, then you're doing it wrong. In researching this book I asked some of the smartest people I know to send me their favourite writings about creativity over the years. Stig Richards, a creative strategist and former colleague, shared with me an essay by science-fiction writer Isaac Asimov: it's a formal submission he wrote after being invited to participate in brainstorms for a US government defence project.[39] The purpose of the sessions were 'to elicit the most creative approaches possible for a ballistic missile defence system'. The sheer creative thinking from the government to invite one of the world's foremost science-fiction writers was a stroke of genius; however, Asimov never actually attended the sessions. Instead he wrote his thoughts down in an essay where he agreed that creativity should be done first individually and then, if necessary, in groups. 'It seems to me then,' he wrote, 'that the purpose of cerebration sessions is not to think up new ideas but to educate the participants in facts and fact-combinations, in theories and vagrant thoughts.' Cerebration sessions? What a lively, underused term that deserves to be popularised and used in honour of Isaac Asimov as a new form of creative ideation for a different generation. Ideas should be celebrated, and I love that it sounds like a fun, smart party full of fun, smart people that I wish I was invited to. So consider this your official invitation to the best new way of coming up with better ideas as a group.

Introducing Cerebrations

Think of ideation sessions like a party: everyone brings presents; there are balloons; and then you open the presents together.

If you're the host of a creative ideation session, you're inviting people to a party and should plan it like one. When you invite someone to a party, the guests know exactly why they're going and what to expect. Think of a Cerebration in the same way: it's an idea party and every guest brings their own thought-starter ideas as presents. You wouldn't turn up to a birthday party without a present, so why would you turn up to a Cerebration without your own ideas?

The aim of a group session is to use divergent thinking to generate lots of different ideas, share your own, make connections with other people's ideas and build on top of all those to try to get from good ideas to a great idea. This session should take place after you've interrogated the problem (Step 1) and then done some of your own thinking on the topic already (Step 2). However, you can't expect that everyone you invite to a group creative session has done the same amount of work, so the beauty of this method is that it compresses each of those two steps into shorter exercises so everyone who shows up can use this process, even if they've done no preparation.

There are three main parts to using Cerebrations as an idea-generating technique, each named after different elements of a party to make it memorable:

1. Blow up balloons.
2. Write out cards.
3. Share the presents.

Yes, you read that correctly. The first step when you arrive to a Cerebration is to blow up the balloons. This is how you come up with killer ideas with a group. Sound like fun? Well, it is!

1. Blow up balloons

Every creative idea is a solution to a problem, but there might be multiple solutions to multiple problems. One way to narrow down your creativity is to focus on one problem at a time. To do that we're going to use the metaphor of a balloon to contain each problem, so start by drawing a giant balloon shape on a wall if you're in a room with other people, or on a digital whiteboard if you're on video conferencing together.

Begin with the primary problem that you're trying to solve (which should be in your brief from Step 1), and think about all the ways this main problem is made up of lots of smaller problems that each ladder up to it. Thinking of it like this gives you multiple entry points into thinking creatively around it, and helps ensure you don't get stuck on just one way in. Put each smaller problem in its own balloon.

This is what it looks like:

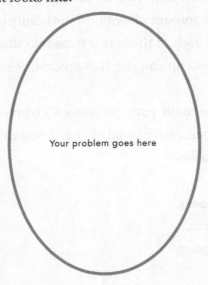

Your problem goes here

Each of these smaller problems will be the focus area for generating ideas, so they should be as broad and open as they can be to encourage people to think about lots of different ways of solving it creatively. Think of three to four smaller problems and write each of them into its own balloon. The problems should arise from the research you did where you have drilled to the core of what you're trying to solve.

To help illustrate this, let's put a hypothetical creative problem into the Cerebration model so you can see exactly how it works.

Primary problem: How do you get more teenagers to eat a healthier breakfast?

As any parents, teachers or older siblings would know, this is a huge problem. Teenagers generally love to sleep in, they usually don't love to spend long preparing their food and they'll often settle for the most convenient, and unhealthy, option if it's easy. So when you begin to think about the different reasons teens might not be eating much in the mornings, or, if they are eating, doing it badly, you can break it down into a series of smaller problems.

When doing a Cerebration session with other people, you should aim to spend about a third of the time understanding the problem. This is the part of the group ideation session where you can share research you've done in Step 1 in getting to know the problem inside out, and begin to formulate the key areas that will make up the bulk of the ideas to be generated.

Depending on the size of the problem you're tackling, and the size of your organisation, five to ten people is optimal for a group creative session, ideally drawn from different departments and levels of seniority. You need to have a firm agenda in order to stop HIPPOs from dominating the conversation. Without it, the loudest voices will automatically fill the voids with their thoughts, so this method gives room for everyone to be heard by forcing the entire group to come up with their own ideas in silence, and then using a random order so no one can command all of the attention.

Here are some examples of the smaller problems that ladder up to our hypothetical example.

Problem 1: *Teens don't have enough time in the morning to make a proper breakfast.*
Problem 2: *Current breakfast options aren't that appealing to teenagers.*
Problem 3: *Teenagers think skipping breakfast stops them putting on weight.*

You can come up with as many smaller problems as you want, but I recommend focusing on the top three to five. This will give you time to go deep into them and come up with lots of ideas. Once you've figured out these problem areas, it's time to 'blow up the balloons' by writing them inside large balloon shapes on a whiteboard or piece of paper. Each problem should be expressed as a question, and should look like the drawings on the following pages.

Balloon 1:

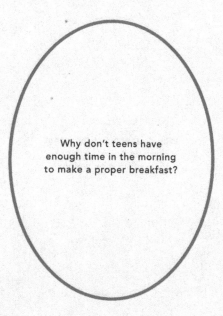

Why don't teens have
enough time in the morning
to make a proper breakfast?

Balloon 2:

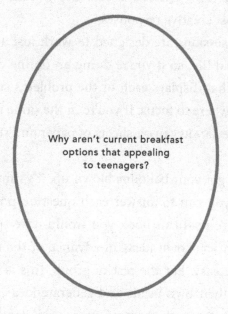

Why aren't current breakfast
options that appealing
to teenagers?

Balloon 3:

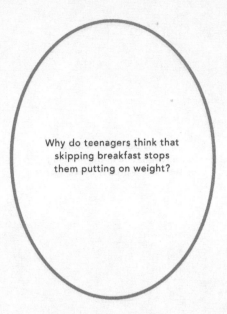

Why do teenagers think that skipping breakfast stops them putting on weight?

The questions inside each balloon should start with who, what, when, where or how. Questions that begin with 'How...?' often generate the most creative responses.

Cerebration sessions are designed to work just as well virtually as they do in real life, so if you're doing an online creative session, share a screen that displays each of the problems so that everyone can see exactly where to focus. If you're in the same room, make the balloons as large as you can on sheets of paper and stick them up on the walls.

Once you've got your balloons blown up, it's time to generate as many ideas as you can to answer each question posed. Of course, because you have read this book you would have spent some time coming up with your own ideas in advance of the meeting, which makes this part easy. For the rest of group, this is their chance to go quietly into their own heads and generate ideas, and you might also come up with some more of your own depending on what inspiration you've just got from blowing up the balloons.

2. Write out cards

Most creative sessions go awry at this point without a clear process to follow. The usual playbook for a brainstorm would descend into idea chaos as thoughts are thrown around at random until something, if you're lucky, sticks. Occasionally it can lead somewhere fertile, but not most of the time.

Instead, the next thing to do in an ideation session is to shut up. Don't share ideas, don't start talking, don't tell people what you think. After the balloons have been drawn up with a problem inside each of them, the aim of the Cerebration is to focus one at a time on each problem.

Think of this like sitting down to write a birthday card. Everyone in the creative session should get their own sticky-note pad, or if you want to save on costs and paper, the note-taking app on your phone will also do the job. Every participant should spend time by themselves coming up with their own ideas, without talking, swapping notes or being influenced by anyone else. Sometimes it helps to spread out around the room, or even in separate spaces if you really want to be alone. This is like an express version of fitting your own mask first before sharing ideas publicly. If you've already done that, use this time to write the ideas down and see if any more can be generated.

Once the primary problem has been established, and smaller problems have been identified that link up to it, everyone in the group should spend some time in silence coming up with solutions by themselves for the issues in the smaller balloons. You should aim to spend five minutes on each balloon before moving on collectively to the next one, but this timeframe can increase if you want people to really go wild. Repeat this until all the problems inside the balloons have been addressed.

Everyone thinks differently, and the point of this private idea-generating is so that a truly diverse range of thinkers can have equal say. During each five-minute period, some people might come up with ten ideas, and others just one. That's OK: there are no wrong levels of contribution here. It might sound counterintuitive to not launch straight into throwing ideas around, but it's important that everyone's voices and ideas get a chance to rise to the surface without the interference of pressure or groupthink.

Every time you come up with creative ideas, there is normally a corresponding thought following right behind to analyse it: *That's silly. That's too expensive. No one would like that. Ugh.* The self-doubting monster will usually rear its ugly head as soon as you think of an idea, and can be bloody distracting if you're trying to deal with it at the same time as coming up with something good. Remember Ed Sheeran's dirty tap analogy? Let every idea flow out, the good and the shit, without editing them. Write them down on sticky notes or pieces of paper, then move on to the next one. Sure, some of them are going to suck, but one of them could also be the start of a killer idea.

Let's return to the example of the primary problem we're trying to solve here, where each of the smaller problem balloons help to do that.

Primary problem: How do you get more teenagers to eat a healthier breakfast?

Balloon 1: Why don't teens have enough time in the morning to make a proper breakfast?

Positioning a problem as a question makes it easier to answer. Follow your thought worms as they lead down different paths to creative ideas. After spending five minutes in silence coming up with ideas, our hypothetical participants offer these answers.

- They sleep too much.
- They have to find clean clothes to wear every morning.
- School starts too early.
- It takes too long to make breakfast each day.

And on it goes.

There are so many different angles to explore. Each area has a rich vein of creative solutions that could generate ideas. It's the job of each participant during the individual idea-generating time to come up with their own creative solutions, writing each one on a new sticky note. Here are some creative thought-starters that someone might come up with.

- They sleep too much.
  *Idea: Educate teens on good sleep hygiene and the dangers of
  oversleeping.*
  Idea: Reward teens who get to bed earlier.
- They have to find clean clothes to wear every morning.
  *Idea: Create a clothing brand using material that absorbs
  smells and never needs to be ironed.*
  *Idea: Encourage schools to have a simple uniform that takes
  the daily clothing choice away from teens.*
- School starts too early.
  *Idea: Team up with schools to provide breakfast for students
  during the first learning session of the day.*
  Idea: Move the start of school back an hour.
- It takes too long to make breakfast each day.
  *Idea: Create a breakfast snack that takes 30 seconds to
  prepare.*
  *Idea: Teach teens how to prepare a week's work of breakfasts
  each Sunday.*

You can see how easy it is to go wild here and come up with lots of ideas. The trick is to focus your creative energy on one balloon at a time, then draw out the answers to each and follow the thought worms to the end to generate ideas around all of them.

You'll find some of them come more easily than others, and that's fine. You should ideally have thought about the problem in advance and possible creative ideas to solve it already in Step 2. If you have, reach into the ideas that have been percolating and draw on them for this process. Enjoy this part; remember that it's meant to be fun!

Repeat the step above for each of the balloons. If you have a few problems to get through, allow five minutes for each one – you should be able to generate a lot of new ideas in that time. The moderator should watch to see how the participants are going with their idea-generating, and move everyone on to the next balloon once they can see that lots of sticky notes have been created.

This step of individually coming up with ideas is one of the rare things that works even better on video conferencing than it does in real life, as it's easy to tune everyone out when you're by yourself with just a computer screen in front of you. At the end of this part, you should have generated lots of individual ideas that are ready to be shared with the other participants.

3. Share the presents

After everyone has generated as many ideas as they can by themselves, it's time to get together and share your presents. This is where we use the power of collective thought to sort through them and begin the process of turning good ideas into killer ones.

Usually a brainstorming session becomes a random chance to yell out ideas, or hold them back if you're more introverted, so the Cerebration model is designed to allow everyone the opportunity to add their idea and be heard. This is the really enjoyable part where people get to share their ideas with the group, and collectively everyone starts connecting ideas, riffing on them and seeing which ideas are the most creative way of solving the problem. Remember earlier when we established that creativity is really about connecting things? The aim of this step is to 'plus' each other and build on top of everyone's ideas.

Start by bringing everyone back into the same room, or onto the same video screen. To avoid the usual HIPPOs dominating the conversation, use this simple trick: go around the group of participants and ask everyone to share their birthdate. The person whose birthday is coming up next, i.e. the soonest possible date after today's date, should be the first person to share their ideas.

Then move around the group running through whoever's birthday is next. This creates a fairly randomised order that changes with the make-up of the group, keeps the same loud voices from always dominating and often changes who goes first depending on when you hold it. It's also a neat trick that works well on video conference calls, and keeps things interesting.

The first person to share their ideas can read out what's on their sticky note and explain it in less than 30 seconds. The key is to keep it short and keep the ideas flowing. Everyone listening should have a pen ready, and write down any new thoughts that are sparked by other people's ideas. The job of the party host or moderator is to group the ideas inside the relevant balloons, with all the ideas that share a similar theme positioned next to or on top of each other. Each person in the group should have a go calling out all of their ideas for each problem, one after another, until the balloons are full of ideas.

Now look at that! In no time, you've been able to generate dozens of fresh ideas that have a chance of starting small and slowly getting refined and combined into a killer idea. Once you've added them all to a physical or virtual whiteboard, each balloon should look something like this (but obviously with a lot more ideas on it):

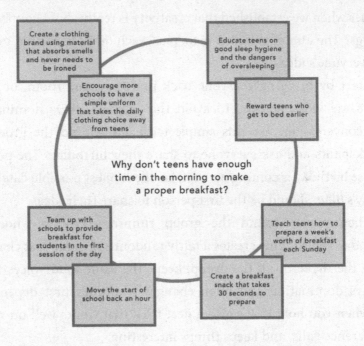

After they are all up on a board together, as a group try to answer the following questions.

- Which ideas stand out the most?
- How can you build on top of these to make them better?
- Which ideas can you connect together?
- Are there any ideas that get you really excited?
- Which idea scares you the most?
- What's an idea you could implement tomorrow?

The aim of this part is to 'plus' each other's ideas. Everyone's ideas should be discussed positively, with one of the ground rules being that everyone must build on someone else's. Sharing your innermost creative thoughts can be scary for a lot of people. Researchers at Google found that the most critical condition in high-performing teams is psychological safety.[40] Behaviours that encouraged this are conversational turn-taking and empathy for other people's opinions and feelings. That's why the Cerebration method has been designed to work in and create a fun and supportive environment.

How you speak in these sessions is very important; language can build or break someone's desire to share ideas every easily. The type of language used should be affirming and encouraging to draw out everyone's ideas equally. There will be time later to edit and refine your ideas until they really pop, so right now you want to extract a multitude of ideas that have all been built on top of each other.

There are two types of language used in creative sessions:

Closed language: Negative phrases that put other ideas down, and subconsciously tell the participants to not share their own ideas.

Open language: Positive words that signal everyone's ideas are valid, and encourage all participants to keep the creativity flowing.

Closed Language	Open Language
But	And
No	Maybe
Instead of that	On top of that
Never	Sometimes
Reasons it would never work	Reasons it could work

Instead of talking over the top of someone by using your own idea as an alternative to theirs, use language like 'and then', 'on top of that' and 'adding to that' to build new ideas and keep the session bubbling away with dozens of fresh thoughts. Killer ideas are born when there's no judgement. This doesn't mean you can't be honest;

it's more about the way honesty is expressed. Ed Catmull, the co-founder of Pixar, wrote in the *Harvard Business Review* that one of his secrets to collective creativity is that 'it must be safe for everyone to offer ideas'.[41] When Pixar show their animated movies as works-in-progress internally, the team ensures there are always fresh eyes in the group and that constructive criticism is welcome. 'We make a concerted effort to make it safe to criticise by inviting everyone attending these showings to email notes to the creative leaders that detail what they like and didn't like and explain why,' Catmull wrote.

Creativity is all about connecting concepts to make something even stronger, so now it's time to have a look at all the ideas written on the whiteboard and see if there are any that can be combined to create an even stronger idea. As the group talks about their favourite ideas, the moderator should put an asterisk next to the most discussed ideas, and encourage interactions from all of the participants.

Being a moderator can be a hard job, but it can also be extremely rewarding. It's a big responsibility to help draw out the best responses, focus attention on key points and ensure the group doesn't go too far off the beaten track. If you are moderating, it's up to you to get everyone involved in the discussion. If one person is talking too much, thank them for their contribution and then ask someone who hasn't spoken up what their opinion is. The conversation is meant to be free flowing, and your aim as the moderator is to keep it flowing in the right direction. Make sure you're keeping a good eye on the time, and move the group forwards if they're stuck on one point by writing it down somewhere and shifting to the next idea.

Returning to our example of generating ideas for teens and their breakfast habits, you could look at combining ideas so you might connect 'create a breakfast snack that takes 30 seconds to prepare' with 'educate teens on good sleep hygiene and the dangers of oversleeping' and come up with a business idea of launching a quick breakfast product that uses its packaging to educate teens on good sleep hygiene. There are so many different ways of connecting ideas until you find something that works.

Josh Howard connected two things to create his own business. He was always obsessed with the technology behind 'just add water' products. It's not a new category – denture tablets have been around for decades, as have stock cubes and powdered cordials – but Josh's idea was to marry this to the global trend for sustainability. 'We're chucking out so much shit all the time – my bin is just full of crap – and think of all the plastic bottles underneath your sink,' says Josh. 'Let's condense and compress the raw ingredients from these products into tablet form so that not only are you saving single-use plastic bottles, you're also helping people minimise their carbon footprints by not shipping water.' Josh founded Single Use Ain't Sexy, a growing company that sells dissolvable hand soap tablets and reusable glass bottles, with a broader vision of selling a full home suite of tablet-based products in the personal care and home cleaning space. 'If you've got anything that's ninety-five per cent water, we're tablet-ising it,' says Josh. It's an example of a business that combined two existing concepts to create something new.

Once you've spent some time talking about the ideas, combining them and highlighting which are the favourites, then you've had a very successful group creative session. The moderator should take photos of the walls, write up some notes as soon as possible after the meeting while it's still fresh, and circulate all the ideas back to the group so everyone can keep thinking about it.

If you've done the Cerebration correctly, you should now have lots of fresh, fragile ideas with the potential to be shaped and refined into killer ones, and that's what we're going to do next.

IRL

Step 3: 'Plus' Each Other's Ideas

Coming up with ideas with colleagues and friends should be fun! Don't forget that when you get frustrated or nothing seems to be working, the Cerebration method will freshen things up and keep you on the right track. We've already run through exactly how to run your own Cerebration session, and you can download free worksheets from timduggan.com.au/killerthinking to make it even simpler.

Exercise 7: Centre the User

It can be easy to lose sight of exactly who your intended audience is for an idea, so this is a bonus exercise you can work on before a Cerebration session to help centre the user at the heart of what you're trying to do. You can do this exercise by yourself or with a group, but let's assume you have convened a group together to come up with some brilliant ideas.

1. Answer these three questions.

Imagine you are the intended audience for this idea. Put yourself in their shoes and answer these three questions. If you're doing this with a group, get each person to answer these individually by taking a few minutes to write them down without talking.

Q1. How does someone feel before this idea exists?
What problem is it solving? What is the emotional state that needs to be fixed – are they frustrated? Scared? Lonely?

Q2. How does this idea help them feel?
Once it becomes a reality, will someone feel more inspired, empowered or relieved?

Q3. So that they can…

Finally, what will this idea help people do once it's out in the world? Will it help someone have more impact or gain more customers, for example?

2. Share your answers.

Once everyone has written down their own answers, go around the group and share them out loud. The moderator should collect all the written answers and circulate them after the meeting.

Feel free to slightly edit the wording of the questions to suit your idea or group. Another variation I've used with the same effect is:

- *A customer comes to us feeling…*
- *We help them feel…*
- *So that they can…*

This simple exercise at the start of any workshop helps to loosen everyone up and remind yourselves to put the end consumer at the centre of your idea. You need to keep them top of mind at all times.

Fast Takeaways

1. Once you've got as far as you can with your own thinking, you need to share your ideas with others to try to create something better together.

2. 'Plussing' an idea means going further with it and giving it that little bit of extra edge to make it really stand out.

3. Brainstorms suck.

4. A better model for group ideation is the Cerebration model that concentrates on individual problem statements, then democratically sharing and building on top of other people's ideas.

5. In a group creative session, you should use open language (phrases like 'building on top of that…') instead of closed language (phrases like 'instead of that…')

Step 4:
Sit with It

All the really good ideas I ever had came to me while I was milking a cow.

Grant Wood, painter

Sit with It

osh Niland has been called the most creative – and controversial – seafood chef in the world,[42] and it all comes down to a simple idea that he has played with and mastered over the past decade: fish should be prepared, treated and eaten the exact same way as meat.

It was an idea that was presented to him as he rapidly worked his way up through kitchens in Sydney and London in his late teens and early twenties. Josh was working at Fish Face, a small restaurant in Sydney's Darlinghurst, when he had a late-night talk with the owner Stephen Hodges after a long service. 'I don't think he remembers much about the conversation.' Josh laughs now as he recalls how he was struggling to keep thinking of new ways to change up the garnishes the fish were served with and to keep the customers, and himself, excited about the menu. 'Think of the fish more as meat,' Stephen told him. 'If tuna looks like a cut of beef, think of it as that… mackerel can be more like a pigeon, and swordfish like a pig.'

Until that point, most fish recipes were pretty standard and overused (lemon or fennel, anyone?) but this deceptively simple thought buried itself inside Josh's head for some reason and wouldn't let go. Every night as he thought up new recipes to add to the constantly changing menu, it swirled around and grew, leading Josh to experiment with new flavours and preparation styles, culminating in the launch of his fish restaurant, Saint Peter, and retail space, Fish Butchery, in Sydney's Paddington, both of which he runs with his wife Julie.

The initial idea to treat a piece of fish exactly the same as a cut of meat pioneered a completely different way of storing, preparing and selling fish. Unlike owners of traditional fish shops, where fish is stored in ice to keep it frozen and cool, Josh believes a wet fish is a bad fish, and that water speeds up degeneration. Instead, Josh hangs and dries each fish in custom-built coolrooms just like meat hanging from hooks.

When Josh first opened his restaurant, instead of using bins to discard fish remains after they were prepared, he laid out a series of trays where everything destined for the garbage was kept and pored over. 'Wastage to me has always been the holy grail of opportunity because – in a Western context – it's always the first thing to get pulled out, usually quite harshly, and then just thrown aside. So, to actually take it out, put it on the bench and really look at it and study it, you can then see all the shapes, sizes, textures and flavours of all of those things.'

Observing and experimenting is when Josh feels most creative and content. He calls it 'the freedom of observation' and loves nothing more than watching new chefs come into his kitchen and building on top of his way of doing something. 'If you have the freedom of observation and use logical thinking, then you can get very expressive and that's the really fun part.' Josh tries to spend as much time in this curious state as he can, allowing his mind to contemplate how other people approach the same fish. 'Watching somebody who's never done it before can often be so amazing,' he explains, 'because you're like, "Well, why did you do it like that?", and they'll say, "Oh, sorry. I didn't know that I wasn't supposed to." And I'll go, "No, that's interesting because you've started on that side and I would have always done it that side," and that might trigger the ability to see something different.'

As well as making delicious food for his customers, Josh is fuelled by the energy of a wider movement to reduce waste and rethink how we engage with excess food. He estimates that around 60 per cent of the entire fish product is thrown away when prepared the usual way, and that's where the opportunity and creativity lies, leading to experiments with methods like dry ageing, offal utilisation and charcuterie. 'By doing that, it creates provocation to a lot of people, both negatively and positively, but in doing so we're coming up with a lot of really good solutions for waste, and that's where the majority of the creativity starts from.'

The best ideas always seem obvious in retrospect, so why hasn't it been done in this way before? Josh points to labour costs (it's time consuming and expensive to cut scales and gut the fish the way they do), and the hierarchical nature of cooking, where seniority is well respected and rarely questioned. 'I think it takes a little bit of courage to get out of the system.'

Josh's first book, *The Whole Fish Cookbook*, was named the Book of the Year at the prestigious 2020 James Beard Awards in the USA. When Josh's second book, *Take One Fish*, was published he returned to visit his mentor Stephen Hodges, who planted the initial idea in his mind during that tipsy late-night conversation. Josh was there to show him how he'd refined that thought over the years, and his new way of breaking down a single fish to utilise up to 90 per cent of it, including the eyeballs, swim bladders and even blood to make black pudding.

Before the reunion, Josh was nervous. He worried this well-respected chef who first taught him how to prepare fish would tell him off for being stupid, or not using the methods he'd passed down. Instead, Josh was shocked by his reaction. The older chef was genuinely blown away by the innovative ways he was using the offcuts that would often be wasted, like making pate from offal. 'Wow. Imagine how many of those bellies and cheeks we threw away back in the day!' Stephen said to Josh. 'This would have saved me so much money if I knew this back then.'

Space, Inputs and Time

If you thought we were going to head straight into refining all the ideas down into just the best ones, you're wrong. In order for the best ideas to rise to the surface, you need to give them room to develop in the background, mostly unconsciously. It might be as you wash your hair in the shower, mindlessly watch TV, or go for a long run. After the Cerebration sessions, there should be a few ideas that stand out above the others. It might be the one that was most discussed during the session, or one that gave you a 'gut feeling' when you first heard it. It could also be the idea that keeps popping back into your head every time you're driving or vacuuming or waiting at the traffic lights. Ideas will fight for attention in your head, and like Darwin's survival of the fittest, the strongest will start to emerge when you give them space to breathe.

Killer ideas rarely arrive fully formed. To allow them ample room to percolate in the dark recesses of your mind, you have to SIT with it. SIT stands for Space, Inputs and Time, and they are the three conditions needed to let the best ideas grow.

Space

Creativity needs room to flourish, an empty room for ideas to bounce around when you're not thinking about them. It sounds counterintuitive, but there's a magic that happens when you create space in the mundane to let your mind wander.

For some people that's the dullness of a long drive, or a half-listen to a podcast as they clean the house. Singer 'Weird Al' Yankovic calls it 'the zombie phase'[43] where he goes into a creative trance and walks around the house for weeks at a time agonising over phrases and word choices for his song parodies.

KeepCup co-founder Abigail Forsyth describes her brain as a big pool of lava. 'I have to swim around in it and then something will bubble up,' she jokes. 'I'm just patiently waiting for that thought to come to the surface and I already intuitively know, yeah, that's what I'll do. You're at your most inventive when your mind is free to just roam around, so it's about creating that space.'

Author Sarah Wilson's main technique for creating space for thinking is hiking. 'Everything works itself out, everything settles... my thoughts get free,' she says. 'I often hike with a piece of paper and a small little pencil down my running bra. I'll stop every now and then and write a couple of words to remind me. I get expansive, excited thoughts when I'm out in nature.'

Sarah is backed up by science, with multiple studies confirming that creative thinking does improve while a person is walking and shortly after. A study at Stanford found that walking boosted creative inspiration.[44]

The theories as to why the simple act of methodically walking helps shift our creative minds into gear are varied. Sarah says one reason walking is so conducive to thinking is due to evolution. 'The reasoned mind, the prefrontal cortex, developed as we became upright humans, when we stopped crawling around on all fours and we got vertical. That rational part of our brain that exists between multiple thoughts and arrives at conclusions is best activated at the pace of walking.'

Hiking is also my favourite way to generate ideas. Almost every weekend, my husband and I lace up our running shoes and head out to explore the forests and mountains around us. With each step I process my thoughts, one foot in front of another. When you don't have to think about anything, you end up thinking about everything, allowing each idea to dart around your brain, chasing after others until you come across one that's so compelling you need to write it down.

Most of this book was written that way. When I finished working full-time at Junkee Media and moved into an advisory role as editor-at-large, Ben and I jumped into a campervan and explored the far corners of Australia for six months. A lot of what you're reading right now was written in the back of a van parked in glorious national parks and at sunny seasides, with the concepts thrashed out in my mind as we hiked. It was the perfect setting to find space to write.

One of my favourite walks on that trip was the Yuraygir Track in northeastern New South Wales, a heavenly slice of 65 kilometres of the state's longest coastal national park. Starting in the small town of Yamba, you walk six hours a day for four full days along mostly sandy beaches. They're the kind of beaches where you can *just* make out the end of the beach curving around in a salty haze in the distance. The best way of tackling it was to give yourself distant but achievable landmarks and reward yourself with a gulp of water or a few mouthfuls of trail mix whenever you reached one. Add in constantly shifting sand under your tired feet and it took about an hour to walk just a few kilometres.

Yet it's one of my fondest memories of the trip. Giving yourself space is to give your mind freedom to actually think. In *Wanderlust: The History of Walking*,[45] Rebecca Solnit writes about this: 'I like walking because it is slow, and I suspect that the mind, like the feet, works at about three miles an hour. If this is so, then modern life is moving faster than the speed of thought, or thoughtfulness.'

There's a Japanese concept called shinrin-yoku that clumsily translates as 'forest bathing'. It basically means spending time in nature and taking it all in through your senses. But in typical Japanese fashion, this idea takes something as ordinary as a bushwalk and gives it a beautiful simplicity.

It's easy to forest-bathe. Listen to the sound of the leaves crunching under the weight of your shoes on your next walk through the woods or park. Notice the calls of the birds chirping above the canopy. Feel the whistle of the wind as it weaves through the trees. It's mindfulness meets mountains, so when you need to find some space to let your thoughts wander, put on your exercise shoes and try walking at the speed of thought.

Inputs

Once you've created space to think, you need to feed the ideas something. Inputs can come in many forms: researching on the internet, reading books, watching documentaries or talking to people with experience who've already made their own mistakes trying to solve similar problems. The more inputs you can add, the better the potential outcome.

The type of inputs you use to fuel creativity doesn't need to be directly related to your problem. Sometimes it's the incidental moments where you might be reading an article in a newspaper, watching a movie mindlessly, or doing something as mundane as preparing a meal that will spark a thought. That's what happened to visionary architect Jørn Utzon as he was contemplating how to best visualise a radical new shape for a building on the edge of Sydney Harbour in the 1960s. 'He sent one of us to the shop to buy an orange,' recalls his chief assistant, Mogens Prip-Buus.[46] 'He peeled it and took apart the segments, and he said, "They are all segments; they are all alike but you can cut them so they are different."' The Opera House's distinctive sails are now included on the UNESCO World Heritage List, alongside the Taj Mahal, the Pyramids of Egypt and the Great Wall of China, as one of the most outstanding places on earth, and it has a small piece of fruit to thank for some of the inspiration.

It mightn't sound like doing something as passive as sitting down to watch TV could help your creative process, but there's real science behind it. Researchers studied the stimulation your brain gets when exposed to other people's ideas and wrote, 'At the neurophysiological level, temporo-parietal brain regions (primarily right-hemispheric) turned out to be particularly sensitive to cognitive stimulation, possibly indicating that cognitive stimulation via relevant memory cues results in a state of heightened focused attention to memory that facilitates efficient retrieval and recombination of existing knowledge.'[47] Or in layperson's terms: reading or watching other people's work can make your own better.

Sometimes just having conversations with people can stimulate creativity. Marc Fennell is a presenter, journalist and writer who has hosted TV shows and panels and created wildly successful podcasts. He carries around a notebook that looks like a child has scrawled dozens of random words on a page and then decided they were in the wrong place and used arrows, circles, squiggles and lines to violently rearrange them. Marc writes in his notebook every single time he has a conversation with someone that sounds interesting. 'I got in the habit quite early on of tracking every idea, no matter how lame or shit or undercooked it is,' he explains of his creative process. 'I write down every idea that comes, and then underneath it I'll write a question mark: Book? Podcast? TV show? Story?'

Lisa Messenger, the author and founder of Collective Hub, feeds her creativity by being 'purposely counterintuitive'. She pushes herself most days to avoid the same routine. 'That can be as simple as if I'm going to walk down to our local coffee shop and I normally go left, then I'll go right,' says Lisa. 'Or if I normally go to a certain bookstore, I'll try one in a different suburb… I try to shake up my neurology every single day and that keeps me creative, open and aware of different opportunities out there.'

Remo Giuffré is the creative supremo behind infamous Sydney retail outlet Remo General Store and the founder of TEDxSydney, one of the most successful offshoots of the global talkfest. He swims most mornings at Bondi Icebergs, an ocean pool carved into the southern end of Australia's most recognisable beach, and relishes the sensory inputs of his ritual walking to the pool. 'For someone who spends a lot of time working on their own,' he says, 'that hour or two in the morning where you're walking with a dog, or from your apartment to the pool and back again, you have so many 30-second interactions and you're hit with so many different visual cues… There is this sparking situation which then is followed by a quiet space of swimming where those things can settle and connect. It's stimulation followed by sensory deprivation, which is kind of an interesting combination for me personally.'

Feeding your brain inputs can be either intentional or accidental, and you need to carve out time for both. I'm at my most creative when I'm travelling. To properly stimulate my most creative ideas, I need to remove myself from my day-to-day and tire my mind out. When you're not walking the same goat tracks every single day, your mind has greater freedom to wander. It's the quiet, unglamorous moments on holidays: a long highway, early mornings in a new bed, the backseat of a taxi, or wandering back streets. They are the moments when ideas ferment into something new.

When Covid-19 temporarily closed international travel, Ben and I started driving up the New South Wales coast in our campervan, and then we kept on driving. We drove into Victoria, then flew to the Northern Territory and Western Australia. Before we knew it, a planned six-week trip turned into six months on the road.

There were so many things to be thankful for during that time, but one of the most unexpected? The sudden flood of creativity that burst back into my life. The usual daily scenes were replaced with new, exciting moments that looked nothing like the day before. Every new stimulus was like an electric shock to my brain, powering a new idea and lighting up neurons that had almost become dormant.

It's not just me who finds travel creatively fulfilling. Julia Busuttil Nishimura is a Melbourne-based cook, author and teacher with a devoted following who adore her fresh take on food that combines her Maltese heritage, love for Italy and her husband's Japanese background in a delicious fusion. 'Creative inspiration comes from lots of different aspects of my life,' she explains. 'For my last book I went to Italy for a month and London and I just got so much inspiration from the markets and from talking to people and seeing how other people cook.

'I get a lot of inspiration from travelling,' she says. 'And a lot of things are from my childhood, memories of growing up from my parents, my grandparents, my Maltese heritage. It all kind of feeds in. It might be things that I very much want to include or things might just pop up. It's a very organic process, really. I don't really have a set, defined way of creating a book or writing... I like the fluidity of it all.'

Even iconic Australian TV show *Kath & Kim* has some advice. After Jane Turner's character Kath Day-Knight wins the first prize in a floral hat-decorating contest, Magda Szubanski's Sharon Strzelecki asks her where she gets her ideas from. 'You know, I just take scenarios from my daily life,' responds Kath, 'vis-a-vis waiting for Telstra to turn up... the fluff from the shower fan...' and even a pineapple that Kath says 'just hit me when I opened the fridge. Literally.'

Time

The last ingredient required to ferment creativity is the only one you don't have much control over. You can create space, you can feed it inputs, but you can't make more time. Often the time needed for an idea to brew in your mind is just a few hours. Or it could take a few weeks, or months or even years depending on the scale of the idea. Time is one of the most important, and neglected, ingredients in creativity, so make sure you schedule in plenty of it to let your killer idea sit.

At the very minimum, every creative idea should be thought about overnight to give it some time. The idea of 'sleeping on it' to involve the unconscious mind is repeated in countless cultures. There are many examples of creativity developing during the half-awake period just after going to bed and right before we wake up. Internationally bestselling author Stephen King says that a lot of his ideas come to him in dreams. One time he fell asleep on the Concord jet on a trip to England and had a dream about a woman who held a writer as prisoner in her house. As soon as he woke, he scribbled his memories of the dream onto a napkin: 'She speaks earnestly but never quite makes eye contact. A big woman and solid all through; she is an absence of hiatus.' (When retelling this story in his book, *On Writing*, he added additional context: 'Whatever that means; remember, I had just woken up!') Rushing off the plane, King checked straight into his hotel and wrote the first 50 pages of the book that would become *Misery*, one of his most famous works.[48]

Research has shown that problem-solving skills improve overnight, especially if you're able to get into the REM dream phase.[49] Let's not kid ourselves and think we can just lazily sleep our way right to a killer idea – however, if you've got a few loose ends that need a creative way of being tied together, sleeping on it might actually be the best next step.

If you don't give yourself time to be creative when you need to be, you can easily end up burnt out or uncreative. It's a lesson that television host and producer Andrew Denton taught filmmaker Kirk Docker when they were working together on the TV show *Hungry*

Beast. Kirk was hired to pitch and make compelling segments, but a few weeks into production he was shooting creative blanks. 'When you're sitting at a desk, there's not much input coming into you from the fluorescent lights,' recalls Kirk.

Andrew pulled him into his office to ask him why his output was not where he thought it was going to be. 'Where are all your amazing ideas?' he asked. 'What happened?' Kirk had to really think about it to find the answer. 'I realised I'd never spent five days in a row in an office on a computer. That's not how I worked,' he recalls. 'I lived five minutes from work, so I was only walking five minutes to work and five minutes home, and I wasn't in the world. I used to be in the car all the time, looking out the window, listening to the radio, letting my mind expand. Just being in the world.' Kirk didn't have any time to actually be creative. His solution was to book in an extra-long overseas trip at the end of each season, 'just to inject myself with life, with ideas, and go away with the sole purpose of finding inspiration.'

Murray Bell, the founder of Semi Permanent, an events company and brand studio, has learnt to give himself time. 'I used to get in this crazy cycle of jumping from meeting to meeting to meeting,' he says. 'And so I started just shifting the way in which I approach things. Now I give myself time. I'll always have at least half an hour between meetings, sometimes more.'

Murray uses the time to think, swim in the ocean if he can or let his mind wander so he can be the best for himself and the partners he works with. 'My most creative time is probably the 15 minutes before I go to bed and 15 minutes before I wake up,' he says. 'It's this beautiful little window where I'm getting sleepy and I can think of some ideas… There's plenty of ideas that are just gone because I've been a bit lazy to write them down. There's a few left on the drawing table but it's one of my favourite times.'

The Beauty in Boredom

Fitzroy is one of Melbourne's most eclectic suburbs. Located just three kilometres northeast of the CBD, it's a mishmash of backpackers, hipsters, students and artists who all share the graffiti-splattered streets. In the thick of it all, Brunswick Street cuts through the suburb, with vintage stores, galleries and dark bars reeking of alcohol and coffee. It was inside one of these institutions, the now-defunct Gypsy Bar, that one of the best charity ideas in the world was born.

Two mates were having a quiet drink in a corner of the bar in 2003. Travis Garone, a gregarious creative with a lifelong affection for Fitzroy, and his mate Luke Slattery, who everyone just calls Lucky, ordered two more Stella Artois beers. Travis was born into a creative family; being immersed into his dad's sign-writing company from a young age instilled within him a natural understanding of business, colour, fonts, typography and design. After study and an initial start to his design career, he quit it all and travelled the world for most of the 1990s, settling in London, Edinburgh, Canada and then in Alaska, indulging his passions for art, culture, surfing and skateboarding wherever he could. Working for small studios and kitchens along the way, he learnt how brands work, how to cook and absorbed culture to gain credibility within communities.

Travis hadn't seen his mate Lucky for almost a decade until they bumped into each other at a skateboarding competition in a Melbourne club. They'd both spent the years moving in similar cultural circles, and once they debriefed on their own adventures realised that somehow they'd ended up in similar headspaces. They agreed to meet up to go skateboarding, grab a beer and catch up on the adventures of life.

Fuelled, in Travis's words, by 'a few quiet beers… no good story starts with a salad', they began unpacking why it seemed like there was nothing much around to help men's health or give men a platform to talk about things that were important to them. They discussed how breast cancer seemed to be quite well understood ('the world seemed to be pink') and the campaigns for it featured quite prominently in media (albeit one of the few areas of women's health where this was the case), but where was the equivalent in the male space? Travis ordered another round, and the conversation switched. They had a friend in the skateboarding scene who had recently grown an impressive moustache.

'Have you seen his moustache?'

'Yes! What the fuck? It's hilarious.'

'Well, have you ever grown a moustache?'

'Listening to myself, it was a bit of a weird conversation, wasn't it?' recalls Travis almost 20 years later. 'There was a big bubbling pot of influences that all went into it.' Their ideas each built on top of each other's: Men's health. Counterculture. Moustaches. Trends. A challenge.

'I wonder how long it takes to grow a moustache?' they wondered, before settling that it would probably take about a month. Travis was planning a party for his birthday at the end of November, and all of the ideas and inputs came together in a fluid, natural way that led them to decide to get some of their mates to grow a moustache for the month.

'Right,' said Lucky, 'and we'll call it Movember.'

'Yep, cool,' responded Travis, not thinking much about it. 'One for the road?'

And so the idea for Movember, men growing moustaches in November for charity, was unceremoniously born inside a small, dingy bar in Fitzroy. Since that simple conversation almost two decades ago Movember has grown into one of the top charities in the world, with well over six million people growing moustaches in 26 official countries to raise more than A$1.5 billion for men's health causes, including mental health and suicide prevention, and prostate and testicular cancer. It's been ranked in the Top 100 best NGOs (non-governmental organisations) worldwide, and named the most innovative not-for-profit organisation in Australia.

And it all began with two mates having a beer and connecting their experiences, then allowing the idea to sit and develop. After that initial drink, Travis and Lucky made a plan to meet up every Sunday to skateboard and build out their idea and vision.

One of the first things they did was create a list of what they wanted to ensure Movember would never become. Almost two decades later, the same list is still used. It included things like the fact they wanted it to remain fun, and to be a charity that is for men and that men could relate to ('We respect women, of course, that goes without saying. We're inspired by the way in which women talk about and act on their health. It was one of the factors that made Movember unique. At the end of the day, it's the women who are key to men's health and the Movember movement. Men's health affects everybody.') They wanted to ensure that any money donated to it didn't get chewed up in administration costs, and for it to be a celebration of men's health. In short, they started to create the essence and DNA of what it would be before they had even fleshed it out properly. 'We wanted to create a movement more than an organisation,' says Travis. 'A platform or forum for guys to do good and have fun, but treat it with the same mentality that we'd treat any other brand that we love, trust and relate to… I wanted to bring [charities] into my world, not go over there.'

This formed the basis for the very first Movember in 2003, when Travis sent an email to some of his mates with the subject line, *Are you man enough to be my man?* Thirty guys signed up to grow a moustache for the month of November, and this all culminated with a party to celebrate Travis's birthday and the freshly grown moustaches. There was no money raised, but the idea got so many people talking and excited that the following year they added a fundraising element and 480 guys grew their facial hair to raise A$54,000 for the Prostate Cancer Foundation of Australia. At the time, that first Movember cheque was the largest single donation the PCFA had ever received.

It's easy to romanticise the founding story, but Travis is keen to bring it back to the reality of why it took off. 'We're not geniuses; we're far from it. Lucky and I had an idea, and it was really clear, we could see it, feel it and we knew what to do,' he says. 'We were young and naive, late twenties, full of bravado and passion and energy, and loved working, we had a raw passion for what we believed in. I love the brand and creative world, the knowledge was there and I had the energy and stupidity. Lucky and I already had successful businesses that we both founded, we knew what we had to do. It was just a perfect combination of people and mindset. Men's health was there for the taking.'

The other main reason for its success is that growing a moustache on your face makes you a 'walking, talking billboard for Movember. It's our ribbon, our badge. The catalyst for conversation,' says Travis. It's hard to not have a conversation with someone about what you're doing when the moustache is on your face, and that proved the key point in virally spreading the message to other people who hadn't heard of it.

Travis is still involved with setting the brand and creative vision and ensuring it stays true to the core principles, while also currently sitting on the board. Over the years he is often asked if he can recreate the success of Movember for other clients. His advice to them? 'Ideas come at any given moment. Embrace them, nurture them… get out of your comfort zone, grab a beer and just throw something out and see if it sticks.'

That might not be the best advice for everyone, but it worked for Travis and Lucky. They got out of their usual environment to let their thought worms develop and percolate. For them it was a dingy little pub in Fitzroy where they sat around and talked about nothing at all, really. You need to break the chains of familiarity and let your mind be exposed to new inputs.

Sometimes, the way to percolate is to just do nothing. Yep: just do zilch, zip, nada. Try instead to make yourself actually bored, because there is a real beauty in boredom that is often overlooked.

We've built our lives to avoid boredom. We've developed a lot of habits to keep our minds busy for every second of the day. It might be podcasts on the drive to work, playing music as we exercise, the television blaring as we cook dinner or scrolling our mobile phones when we're on the toilet. We spend a lot of time, and money, so we don't get bored. And why is that? Some people don't like being alone with their own thoughts, perhaps worried where they might go. But the more time we spend avoiding what's inside our heads, the bigger a problem it becomes. Being bored forces thought worms to squeeze through the holes created by the lack of stimulus.

Call me weird, but I love being bored. I often go out of my way to try to make myself as bored as I possibly can. When I was in my late twenties I even spent a few weeks alone on a desert island just to see what would happen. For years I'd fantasised about taking time out to climb up Maslow's hierarchy of needs until I reached the peak and could self-actualise all day without any distractions. I wanted to see what would happen if I got genuinely, totally, hopelessly bored.

I put in my backpack food, a tent, clothes and not much else. There were no books to read. No music to listen to. Nothing to distract me from myself. What would happen when my mind began wandering off with nothing left to tether it to? Would I go mad? Would I have a breakthrough or a breakdown? Could I get bored of boredom? The only item I allowed myself as a creative outlet was a notepad and a pen so I could record some of my thoughts (it's a story for another time that I somehow managed to lose both the notepad and my camera on the journey home).

To help pass the time on the island I counted, then re-counted, the number of zips on my jacket (answer: 44), I began singing to myself just to check my voice box still worked (spoiler: it did), I built fires then extinguished them, and I spent entire afternoons just lying in my tent staring up at the shadows dancing on the walls, creating stories about them inside my head.

In short, I got really, really bored.

I also got creative. Instead of the usual distractions of everyday life, where thoughts collide with each other in quick succession (those pesky 6,200 thoughts a day), I had long stretches of time to just mull over ideas. They were the seeds of the thoughts that would help me launch, grow and sell my business over the next decade. Once my mindset flipped on the island, I relished the chance to have nothing to think about. The solo time fed my thought worms until they became fat and thick.

I also realised you don't need to isolate yourself on an island to get bored. You just need to turn off some of the inputs into your brain by consciously switching off and slowing down: going for a long walk without switching on a podcast, driving without radio, or swimming where technology can't follow you into the water. That's the soft space we need to percolate our ideas. Without it, our jumbled, messy thinking has no room to process itself.

Boredom is the mother of creativity, and you need to work all the way through it until you get to the other side. The Turner

Prize-winning artist Anish Kapoor called boredom 'the cloud of unknowing' and willingly spends time chasing down dead ends to create his sculptures.[50] 'It is precisely in those moments when I don't know what to do and boredom drives one to try.'

When you're bored you're not thinking about anything else, and you give your mind the freedom to daydream. Harvard psychologists Daniel Gilbert and Matthew Killingsworth developed an iPhone app that contacted over two thousand people at random times throughout the day to find out if their minds were focused on what they were doing or if they were daydreaming.[51] Their 2010 study found that we let our minds wander 47 per cent of the time that we're awake. In fact, according to their study, the one time our minds were not constantly wandering? Love making. That's the one time we're able to properly focus on just the task at hand.[52]

Give yourself permission to wallow in the unknowing. Consciously plan ahead to do nothing; add some boredom time into your calendar and see where your mind takes you. It's in those quiet, unassuming moments we fight so hard to avoid that the real magic happens.

IRL

Step 4: Sit with It

You can't rush creativity, and this is probably the most important step out of all of them. It's also the one that's hardest to control, but by giving yourself space, new inputs and time, you're allowing yourself the best chance of coming up with something truly great.

Exercise 8: SIT Plan

Create a personalised plan to figure out what Space, Inputs and Time are best suited to you. To do this, you need to think about your situation and where you feel the most creative. Just writing it down can help you identify and connect deeper with both incidental and intentional places.

1. Draw up three columns with the headings 'Space', 'Inputs' and 'Time'.

It should look like this:

Space	Inputs	Time

2. Answer the following questions.

In each column, fill out your response as bullet points and use each prompt as a way of thinking about how each answer makes you feel.

Space:

- Where do you feel most creative?
- When was the last time you had lots of good ideas?
- Is there somewhere you can go to be completely alone?
- How can you minimise technology and other distractions?
- Where do you feel super comfortable?

Inputs:

- What media can you consume that's (even tangentially) related to your topic?
- Who can you speak to who might give you fresh angles to explore?
- Can you schedule any long road trips or travel any time soon?
- Is there any research you can do to help fuel ideas?
- Where do you record any ideas that come to you at strange times?

Time:

- How long does it usually take you to process your thoughts?
- What can you do to get better sleep?
- When was the last time you were bored?
- Are you giving your ideas long enough to percolate?
- How can you carve out time in your schedule to think?

Once you've filled in each of the columns with answers to the above questions, you should hopefully see some themes emerging. You should aim to have one main takeaway from each column that you can incorporate into your life.

> **Space:** What's the one place I can reliably go to and be creative?
> **Inputs:** Which data do I need to get inspiration?
> **Time:** Where is the space in my calendar to be creative?

Answer each of those questions and you have the basics of a plan to let good ideas sit and develop into truly great ones.

Exercise 9: The Boring Exercise

This is the most boring exercise in the book. It's intended to be that way and help you add boredom into your schedule. It's hard to be bored, but it's also a time when your mind will be free to fill in the blank spaces with unexpected ideas. Want to get bored?

1. Clear at least an hour in your diary.
In our modern lives, with instant access to information and entertainment at our fingertips whenever we need it, it's actually hard to be bored. So you need to dedicate time to it and schedule at least an hour in your diary to do absolutely nothing. Start off with an hour, and slowly build up the length of time that you intentionally disconnect from the world.

2. Turn all of your devices off.
That means everything: your phone, computer, wearables, TV, podcasts, radio, all of it. Switch it off completely and put it away. You don't want any distractions. If this makes you anxious, you can use your phone to set a timer for your allocated time, but that's about it.

3. Instruct others not to disturb you.

A lot of our distractions come from well-meaning colleagues, family and friends, so if you can, let them know you're going to be offline for a while. They should respect what you're doing and give you the space and time to be bored. This can also give you peace of mind that you're not going to miss anything earth-shattering or they will let you know.

4. Choose a distraction-free environment.

Where you decide to get bored is different for everyone. Some might prefer an empty bedroom, others a verandah overlooking a view. I like to move when I get bored, so I might aimlessly wander a park near my house with my noise-cancelling headphones on with no sound in them. This helps me block out the rest of the world. Choose a place that works for you and, well, don't do anything. Get bored.

5. Write down key thoughts.

You need an outlet to take the thoughts out of your head so you can create space for other ones. Bring a small notepad so you're not tempted to write out pages and pages of thoughts. Writing down bullet points of the ideas that come into your head allows your mind to keep rotating through new thoughts knowing you have captured them.

And that's it. You're going to get some weird thoughts floating into your head. That's the beauty of boredom.

Fast Takeaways

1. In order for the best ideas to rise to the surface, you need to give them room to develop in the background, mostly unconsciously.
2. Great ideas develop when you SIT with it (SIT stands for Space, Inputs and Time, and they are the three conditions that let the best ideas grow).
3. At a bare minimum, every creative idea should be thought about overnight to give it some time.
4. Most people try to avoid boredom, but it's one of the most fertile ways to foster creativity.
5. You should consciously plan to add some boredom time into your calendar and see where your mind takes you.

Step 5:
Apply the Right Filter

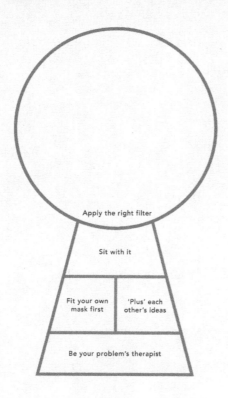

Apply the right filter

Sit with it

Fit your own mask first

'Plus' each other's ideas

Be your problem's therapist

Creativity is a wild mind
and a disciplined eye.

Dorothy Parker, writer

Apply the Right Filter

The best ideas don't arrive fully formed; they need to be massaged, tweaked and refined to make them better. If you give up too early in the process you can miss out on the full potential of a great idea.

That is something Becky Richards knows all about. In 2006 Becky was the adult clinical services director at Kaiser South San Francisco Medical Centre. This one hospital alone administered 800 medications a day to patients, most of them delivered by nurses making their rounds and trying not to make any mistakes. But sadly, mistakes did occasionally happen. It's been estimated that nurses make an error roughly one out of every 1000 medications that are administered.[53] In a hospital like Kaiser South, that's around 250 errors a year that could turn out to be deadly, and up to 400,000 people a year in just the United States.

It was a big problem that needed a big solution. Surely there was a way of using technology, data and processes to solve it? The nurses on the front line at Kaiser South thought long and hard and came up with lots of ideas, like creating special procedures for administering serious drugs such as morphine and insulin. They tried them all with little success.

But Becky had an idea. She began by thinking about the environment the nurses were working in. Traditionally, hospitals put the areas where medications are administered right in the middle of the nursing unit, which tends to be the loudest and most distracting part of the ward. When nurses make their rounds to dole out medications to patients, they are constantly interrupted by anyone who sees them walking past – patients, doctors and other nurses. It's no wonder so many mistakes are being made, thought Becky, everyone is getting distracted all of the time.

Her solution to this was a good idea: the nurses could wear something that would signify they were on a medication round and shouldn't be disturbed. Compared with the complicated procedures and processes, it wouldn't cost much and was easy enough to implement.

They considered different types of clothing like aprons and armbands, and eventually settled on a vest. Becky ordered some online and a week later a few dozen cheap bright-orange plastic vests arrived. The nurses in two of the units were given an explanation of how the test would work: every time they administered medications, they were to put on the vest, and if they saw someone wearing the bright-orange vests, they would leave them alone.

For the next few months, the nurses wore the vests when doing their rounds, and they all kinda hated it. Their complaints piled up: they couldn't find the vest when they needed it, they looked 'cheesy', they were hot and itchy, and the nurses felt it was demeaning. They also reported back that the bright vests seemed to have the opposite of their intended effect and attracted more attention to them doing the rounds, rather than less. The feedback was pretty brutal, but still they persevered throughout the study. A lot of people were ready to give up on the idea. 'We were really thinking about abandoning the whole idea, because the nurses did not like it,' Becky told RN.com.[54]

Then the results came in.

The two units that trialled the vests for five months combined had a 47 per cent decrease in medication errors. They hadn't changed anything else in their procedures; they'd just worn the vests. The hospital and nurses were shocked that such a small change could have a big effect. 'At that point we knew we could not turn our backs on our patients,' said Becky.

The nurses set about refining the idea to make it better, taking into account all the feedback from their teams. They tweaked the colour from construction-style orange to yellow, improved the quality of the material so it didn't itch, and designed a specific location in the wards so they were always available in the same place whenever nurses needed to find them.

In 2007 most of the rest of the Kaiser South team implemented the medication vest program. From there, the success of the program saw it taken up and adapted all over the world. Some wards now use a sash instead of a vest, and the thinking has evolved into a wider education practice about the importance of an interruption-free environment that uses the idea of 'no disruption vests' as its centrepiece. And the results? They are beyond impressive: a multi-hospital study conducted over three years coordinated by the University of California found an 88 per cent drop in the number of errors.[55]

All that because a few nurses had a simple idea for a big problem. Their first idea was good, but by the time it had been tested in real life, experimented with and tweaked, it became a killer idea that, yes, ironically, helped save thousands of lives every year.

Select the Best Ones

By this stage, you should have a few good ideas you've asterisked as having potential, and now you can refine them to make them better. This is where divergent thinking flips into convergent thinking, as the wide list of possibilities is narrowed down to the best ones. This is a conscious process in which the free-flowing river of creativity meets a clear-headed logic and you need to assess each idea on its merits. It's an important mental shift to make, and something a lot of creatives find difficult.

Actor Lou Gossett Jr won an Oscar for his portrayal of Sergeant Emil Foley in the 1982 film *An Officer and a Gentleman*. Playing opposite Richard Gere, he was one of the original villains on screen: a hard-driving, trash-talking, take-no-prisoners military officer who puts his recruits through hell to test their limits. Comedian Jerry Seinfeld says you need to be 'just a hardass' and channel that character when you get to the filtering stage. 'The key to... being a good writer is to treat yourself like a baby, extremely nurturing and loving,' he told a podcast,[56] 'and then over to Lou Gossett in *An Officer and a Gentleman* and just be a harsh prick, a ball-busting son of a bitch. "That is just not good enough! That's got to come out, or it's got to be redone or thrown away!" Flipping back and forth between those two brain quadrants is the key to writing.'[57]

To channel your inner critic you need a clear filter. Think of it like sifting through flour: in order to get the best, most refined flour you've got to put it through a sieve that's built for exactly that reason. Your filter will help you sort out the best ideas from the rest, and provide clear parameters within which to measure ideas against each other. To do this, we'll return to the initial brief you created in Step 1 to ensure the filter meets all the right criteria. For example, there's no point coming up with an idea that will cost a million dollars to execute when your budget is one thousand dollars.

A clear filter will stop you wasting time on the wrong projects. In the late 1990s, two software co-workers often carpooled together from their homes in Santa Cruz, California, to their offices in Silicon Valley. During the hour-long commute, they would share business ideas they were thinking about, using their own filters to determine whether it was worth leaving their jobs to build something with each other. One of their first ideas was personalised shampoo. Customers would cut off a lock of their hair and mail it to the company, where a team of hair scientists would formulate a custom shampoo just for you. Another idea was for custom pet food, created for the specific breed, gender and age of the animal. The ideas were interesting, but the carpoolers' analytical minds were able to find all the holes in each of the potential businesses. Finally, after months of travelling together and dozens of ideas, one of them pitched an idea to the other: renting video movies through the mail. 'That's the stupidest thing I've ever heard,' the other one responded immediately. 'That will never work.'

Despite the initial gut reaction, there was enough interest for them to continue to explore this idea further, patch up the holes in the business model and expand the vision of what it could be. The carpooling co-workers? Marc Randolph and Reed Hastings, who went on to launch their company, Netflix, in 1997.[58]

The right filter for your ideas depends on what you're trying to achieve. Set the purpose of what you're trying to solve, and then use that as a criterion to decide if an idea works or not. This might change with every problem you're trying to solve, but if you want to create a killer idea, you need to have a killer filter. It's a way of ensuring that any ideas have the potential to do some good in the world, and spread to a point where they are able to have a deep positive impact.

A Killer Filter

To decide which ideas have the most potential to be truly killer ones, the best creative thoughts you have should be evaluated via the following questions, using the framework we introduced earlier in the book as a guide.

Kind:
- Is it kind to the world in which it operates?
- Does it help the environment, the community it serves, its suppliers and its audience?
- Does it make the world a slightly better place because it exists?

Impactful:
- Does it have a big impact in its intended area?
- What effect could it have if all went to plan?
- Is it worth the effort?

Loved:
- Is this an idea people might adore?
- Will people love this idea so much they'll tell others?
- Is this an idea someone will really identify with?

Lasting:
- Does the idea have the ability to run for a long time?
- Is it adaptable as its environment or audience changes?
- Will people easily bore of the idea?

Easy:
- Can it be easily communicated in a single sentence?
- Is the idea as simplified and as streamlined as possible?
- Can people pass it on to others easily?

Repeatable:
- Does the idea have the ability to be repeated over and over?
- Is the idea one that can generate its own momentum?
- Will people *want* to talk about their experience with other people?

The KILLER Filter is a useful tool with which to evaluate your ideas, but you should also create your own criteria for what success looks like to you. One way of doing this is by using the 'Essentials' section of the creative brief as a way of determining if an idea will work or not.

Essentials
These questions will be customised to your specific idea and based on your initial brief. The mandatory elements could be anything from the size of the budget available to the location the idea needs to be implemented in or how long you've got to bring it to life. This connects the final ideas with the aim and intention of the creative brief.

A filter will offer big questions for you to decide if your idea is good enough at the moment. If the answer to some of them is a clear no, think about whether there's a way you can refine the idea even further to make it more kind, repeatable, or easy to understand. In the IRL section at the end of this chapter you'll find a downloadable worksheet you can fill out to apply this filter to your ideas.

Switching from divergent to convergent thinking can be hard. Coming up with ideas is the easy part compared to viewing them in the harsh light of day and deciding which ones are the best to focus on: the ideas that can actually be brought to life.

Take the example of naming new projects and ideas. When we were coming up with ideas for the name of our youth-focused pop culture title, launched in 2013, we had a list of essentials:

1. Be memorable to stand out in a crowded field.
2. Reference pop culture in some way.
3. Be able to register the .com domain.

We spent hours throwing names around, writing them up on a whiteboard, sitting with them and putting them through the filter. The name of the website alone wasn't big enough of an idea to apply the full KILLER filter, but we applied the list of 'essentials' that were mandatory for our creative thinking. We ran through dozens of names, playing around with variations, until we landed on our final top two: The Drop and Junkie. At the time there was a trend for things to be named 'The Something' (even Facebook was initially called The Facebook), and we liked it because it felt like the name of a cool indie band. But the other potential title, Junkie, had a strong reference to being a 'pop culture junkie', and getting your fix of entertainment news. It was really difficult to choose which name to go with, so we ran them both through the filter we had created:

1. Be memorable to stand out in a crowded field.

   ✗ The Drop: Lots of bands, songs and websites start with 'The'.

   ✓ Junkie: The name jolts you awake, and not many brands start with 'j'.

2. Reference pop culture in some way.

✓ The Drop: You get a drop of information, new music and gossip.

✓ Junkie: Pop culture or movie junkie is a common phrase.

3. Be able to register the .com domain.

✗ The Drop: The domain was registered in 2001.

✗ Junkie: The domain was registered in 1998.

You can see that when we applied the filter, it was clear Junkie was the name that better fulfilled our list of requirements, but we couldn't get the domain name for it as someone was already using that URL. As an online media title, a short and memorable domain was a key part of our marketing and audience strategy, so we needed to come up with another solution. Eventually someone in the room suggested we just spell it differently. That way we could keep the sound of the name, and end up making it even more memorable by misspelling it. We liked the uniqueness of Junkee.com, which had already been registered by cyber squatters, and paid A$7,500 to take it off their hands to become the new home, and name, of our soon-to-be-launched website, Junkee.

Filter, Refine and Repeat

Julia and Jordy Kay don't like to waste any time, in business or in their personal lives. Three months after meeting at a rooftop bar in Fitzroy, Melbourne, and starting a relationship, they launched a business together. Six months later, they were engaged to be married. On one of their dates they were walking on a beach talking about the wastage in pallet wrapping (as you do). As an organic winemaker, Jordy mentioned he was wrapping lots of large pallets for wine production, and Julia, an architect, saw the same thing in construction.

As this waste was such a common problem in both of their fields, they wondered aloud why no one had come up with a better solution. Julia and Jordy saw that a materials revolution was happening around them. So many things were changing rapidly... except for plastic. It continued to be wrapped and wrapped and wrapped around manufacturing products with a one-time use.

They resolved to understand every inch of the plastic problem. They researched extensively, and saw that Australia alone sends 150,000 tonnes of pallet wrap and cling wrap to landfill every year. They discovered that 10 per cent of the world's petroleum is used to make plastic, and that it is currently much cheaper to make pallet wrap from virgin plastic than to recycle it. Instead of being scared of or paralysed by the mounting problem in front of them, they saw it as an opportunity to disrupt an old industry and help the world dump plastic once and for all.

They started by attacking the problem from all angles, sorting through ideas until they got to the right one. Their first idea was to see if they could change the process of industrial-scale plastic wrapping by creating a reusable pallet system, like a clip or something similar, that could be used over and over. They toyed around with some ideas but realised that it's difficult to change people's habits, and a better approach instead was to work within the existing system by updating the material.

Then they began a long stretch of experimentation: they purchased existing products and materials, and found others that were biodegradable but not compostable. They read books, chatted with university professors, met with the Australasian Bioplastics Association, studied scientific papers and conducted a lot of testing using trial and error.

Julia and Jordy researched their problem and potential solutions for 18 months before deciding on a test formula, then took another six months to launch their first product. Great Wrap was a new type of plastic film available in two variations: a business product they would sell as pallet wrap to corporations, and a product for consumers looking to buy sustainable cling wrap for their homes. They tested the market with a 'really horrible website' and, after a few launch social posts about their new plastic wrap, they basically sold out. 'Everyone was so excited, and just going crazy about it,' says Julia.

The product was initially made using cornstarch. It was a step up from the use of oil in the production of most cling films, but the more they learnt about the intensive agricultural process behind the farming of cornstarch, they soon realised the amount of chemicals, pesticides and water that went into developing the resin meant it wasn't actually a sustainable product. 'The first iteration of a product doesn't always go to plan,' says Jordy. 'That was a very painful lesson.' They had to rethink the product from the ground up. They searched for better material and eventually settled on diverting food waste from landfill and converting it into their main ingredient. They therefore minimise the amount of methane they're adding to the atmosphere, as they're using a waste product that doesn't involve intensive agriculture – and removing material that would otherwise create even more methane to warm the planet.

Within 18 months of launching Great Wrap, they had removed over one million metres of petroleum plastic from our landfills, waterways and parks. Their consumer cling wrap is their front-facing product, but the real impact will come from industrial-use pallet wrapping, used by companies all over the word – they aim to revolutionise how the manufacturing industry approaches plastics and entirely change the future of packaging. 'It feels like the world is burning and there's this finite piece of time that you've got to reverse this horrible destruction we're causing from a sustainability aspect,' says Jordy. 'So with what we're doing, it's a race, and we have to be the biggest and the best. We have to do it because someone else will do it and they'll do a shit job and completely ruin this opportunity to change this material.'

Jordy and Julia started with a good idea: to create a sustainable alternative to plastic wrapping. Their first iterations were a step in the right direction, but they didn't tick off enough boxes in making it kind to the environment. So they scrapped it and searched for better ways to do that. They view plastic packaging as a spectrum, encompassing all of the possible solutions for the problem of waste as concepts. As their idea has evolved, they have moved their business along the scale. 'Constantly improving on what we're doing is a big part of why we've got to where we are so far,' says Julia. 'It's not like we just arrived at a product and it was done.'

The best ideas might appear effortless, but it takes a lot of refining, filtering and work to get it there. Take *You Can't Ask That*, which looks like the easiest television show in the world to make. Created by Kirk Docker and Aaron Smith, it features people from all walks of life sitting on a stool answering confronting questions submitted by the audience. 'Is dwarf tossing OK if the money's good?', 'Why are you so fat?' and 'Have you had *the* surgery?' are just some examples of the questions asked of short-statured people, fat people and transgender people, and many more marginalised or misunderstood groups such as suicide attempt survivors, former cult members, recent war veterans and ex-reality-TV stars.

On the surface, the concept seems so straightforward that anyone can do it. They put up a mottled grey sheet, people sit in front of it and are asked questions you're not supposed to ask. Kirk says people always come up to him and say, 'Oh, I wish I'd come up with that idea; it's so simple.' But like most things that seem easy from afar, the reality is quite different. 'There's so much thought behind every decision that has gone into that show,' says Kirk. 'Every single thing that happens in that show happens for a very particular reason.'

Take the interview background: a plain sheet the filmmakers can pack into a bag and take anywhere in the country with just two people. It means they can shoot in a hotel room, a boardroom or a studio and the look is instantly recognisable as being the same show. Or that every participant is positioned on the same stool. Not a chair, or standing, but a plain stool. 'The stools are about performance,' says Kirk, who has purchased the stools all over the country so they don't need to pack them onto a plane.

There's also the text that appears onscreen at seemingly random times to emphasise certain points. The words appear as a representation of a barrage of noise from 'the outside world' that the participants have to hear endlessly in their lives. Even Kirk's role as the interviewer is invisible and off-camera, designed to heighten the sense of a conversation between the audience and the person on the stool. 'We didn't want my voice in it,' he says. 'This is about giving all the dignity over to the person with lived experience, giving voice to the voiceless... Normally when there's discourse around these sorts of ideas, these people are the last people who actually get a voice. You've got your expert talking, or friends and family or politicians talking. So this was a really important decision to...

have this person talking down the barrel to the audience.'

The directors commission original music for every episode and they made the creative decision to not reveal the names of the participants until the end, as they don't want the audience looking them up and reading their stories before they've had a chance to explain them themselves.

Those small decisions come together to add up to something special: an innovative and flexible TV format that has now become one of the ABC's most successful ever.[59] It's one of the most fascinating and insightful shows on TV, and an idea that ticks the boxes of the KILLER filter, refined over time.

Kind

The aim of the show is to encourage empathy for and understanding of other people's lives, with genuine diversity at its core. 'People are voyeuristic, they want to understand people, but they don't necessarily have the skills to go about it,' says Kirk, 'so we provide that for them.' Kirk and Aaron have perfected their storytelling over the years to let the participants shine even brighter.

Impactful

The show has consistently high ratings in most of the markets it's produced in, and was named as one of the world's hottest TV formats in K7 Media's list of the top 100 unscripted TV formats in 2021.[60] Kirk gives guidance to each market to make it local and relevant. 'What are the touchpoints in your country?' he asks them. 'What are the topical issues that need to be spoken about in your country right now?'

Loved

The show has built up a dedicated fan base globally, with high ratings when the episodes are aired on television, and even higher view counts on social media as people engage with short, emotional clips from the show that are built for sharing. It was awarded a coveted Rose d'Or for the Best Reality and Factual Entertainment Program in the world in 2017.

Lasting

The show has been renewed on the ABC every year since 2016, expanding internationally; and given the endless list of potential topics and its ongoing popularity, there's no reason we'll see it slowing down any time soon. *You Can't Ask That* now consists of 35 seasons filmed in 11 countries and nine different languages.

Easy

The best ideas are very easy to understand, and *You Can't Ask That* can be explained in a single sentence. This has helped it to translate into several cultures, and the seemingly simple structure of the show has been tweaked over seven seasons to be instantly recognisable. Kirk and Aaron have spent a lot of time refining the idea down to its purest form. 'What's that one liner? What's that simple sell? Can someone explain it to someone else? I think that's ultimately the trick,' Kirk says. 'They need to be able to summarise it succinctly so they can recommend it, and they need to be able to do it in a way that's compelling, so the other person's sold on it.'

Repeatable

You Can't Ask That is relevant in every market it's repeated in, a real sign of the strength of the idea. 'Anyone can sit on the seat,' says Kirk. 'Every country has misunderstood people... every person in the world judges other people and has questions they want to answer, and this is constantly changing as the world changes. So it can go on forever if you really want to keep making it.'

IRL

Step 5: Apply the Right Filter

The switch from coming up with lots of ideas (divergent thinking) to narrowing down to the best ones (convergent thinking) is hard for some people to make. You need a really clear way of deciding which ones you should home in on and focus energy towards, and that's where a great filter comes in. You can download free templates that are pre-filled with a KILLER filter from timduggan.com.au/killerthinking or you can create your own using the same template. Every idea is unique, and your filter should be too.

Exercise 10: The KILLER Filter

This filter will help you narrow down good ideas into better ones. It uses the framework of KILLER, as well as the addition of requirements that were 'essential' to your idea that you added to the creative brief all the way back in Step 1.

1. Draw up a table on a piece of paper for each idea you have.
Download this template or recreate the table so that it looks like this.

Idea:	Yes	No	How?
Kind			
Impactful			
Loved			
Lasting			
Easy			
Repeatable			
Add Your Essentials			

2. Add your personalised list of 'Essentials'.

Every idea you have is unique, and you would have developed a list of mandatories during the creative brief. Add them into the table so you can evaluate each of the ideas by how well they tick all the boxes.

3. Run each idea through the filters.

For every idea that's made it this far, write down where it sits on each of the attributes. Is it kind? Impactful? Loved? Tick the 'yes' or 'no' column, and then write the reasoning behind your answer. Explain things like 'Why do you think the idea has potential to be loved?' or 'How is this idea repeatable?'

4. Think through how to turn the 'no' answers into 'yeses'.

If the answer for each filter is 'yes', then that's awesome. If the answer is 'no', what can you do to modify the idea so that it's kinder, more impactful or easier to understand?

This exercise will help people not only filter their ideas, but begin the process of moving them along the quality scale, which we'll explore in the next step.

Fast Takeaways

1. The best ideas are constantly tweaked and refined to make them better.
2. You have to consciously transition from divergent thinking (generating ideas) to convergent thinking (selecting the best) or you won't be able to focus.
3. A clear filter for ideas will stop you from wasting time on the wrong projects.
4. To create a killer idea, you need to apply a filter to test whether an idea is kind, impactful, loved, lasting, easy and repeatable.
5. The criteria you use to assess your ideas can be customised based on the mandatories or 'Essentials' you outlined in your original creative brief.

Step 6:
Stretch It Out

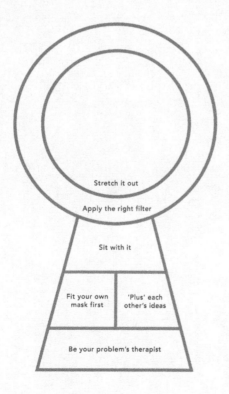

Stretch it out

Apply the right filter

Sit with it

Fit your own
mask first

'Plus' each
other's ideas

Be your problem's therapist

One thousand days to learn; ten thousand days to refine.

Japanese proverb

Stretch It Out

When Mike Smith sold one of the first businesses he co-founded, a contemporary wine company that shook up a traditional industry, he packed up his life and spent a few years travelling the world with his wife. Instead of heading to the well-trodden haunts of Europe and America, however, they trekked throughout much of the Middle East, Russia and along the borders of Afghanistan, Iran and Iraq. They even managed to explore parts of North Korea together. 'We went to some really crazy places,' he says. 'It was the most amazing two years of my life.'

While travelling, Mike couldn't help but notice the obscene amount of rubbish in remote wilderness locations. It's sadly expected that densely populated cities are already overflowing in rubbish, but seeing it in some of the most isolated villages on Earth really affected Mike. 'I said to myself, "Okay, when I go back to Australia, I'm going to start a company that's going to try and solve this problem," as audacious as that sounds.'

Mike had found a big problem that motivated him, and spent some of his time away interrogating it deeply. He brought a few insights back home with him. The first was that the current way of trying to solve the pressing global problem of waste wasn't working.

Governments and big business had both failed. 'We've been debating the climate measures that need to be implemented at a national level for 30 years now, and they're still not being implemented, so I ruled out government as the answer to solve this problem,' says Mike. 'There's also no incentive for big business to solve this, because it adds extra costs and requires them to re-engineer their entire supply chain.' The solution, he theorised, was a community-driven, people-powered movement started by small businesses that can grow into bigger businesses as more people support them.

Mike now had a problem, and the insights, but what he didn't have was an obvious solution, so he experimented with a few ideas first. One of the first iterations he explored was a food business that tackled the issue of plastic packaging in supermarkets. 'Every loaf of bread comes in a single-use plastic bag, and every packet of pasta is in a single-use plastic bag,' says Mike, who valiantly thought he would start with one of the biggest categories of plastic wastage in the world. He put together a slide deck to get other people on board and did lots of research. But the more he looked into the problem the more he realised how challenging it would be to make an impact, given the area of food standards and supply chains is highly regulated and incredibly complex.

It was while researching this idea that Mike stumbled onto another one, in the next aisle of the supermarket. The personal-care and home-cleaning category is a multi-billion-dollar industry, dominated by the same global players for decades. 'I just had a kind of "Aha" moment when I realised how big the category was,' says Mike. 'And those aisles are floor-to-ceiling, wall-to-wall, single-use plastic... Laundry liquid has been the same for decades and decades and decades. Omo has been in the same blue bottle, there's been little innovation to the product, the packaging, or from a brand and communications perspective.'

Based on his previous business experience, Mike knew he had the skills to make the product and packaging better and more environmentally friendly with his company Zero Co. 'I'm going to make the products look sexy and objects of desire in the home,' he said. 'I'm going to go and change the way that you talk about this category, and make it fun and irreverent and relatable to a new generation of people who, to be quite frank, don't give a fuck about Omo, but they have come to give a really big fuck about Zero Co because of everything we're doing.'

Zero Co has a unique distribution system to reduce single-use plastics of common household products like washing powder and dishwashing detergent packaging by using a circular system whereby products are delivered direct to consumers in refillable pouches. The product is poured into 'Forever Bottles' that live in customers' houses, and the pouches are returned to be refilled over and over.

Mike was excited: he could see the vision, and he set about pitching his new business to every venture capital fund and accelerator that he could. Every single one of them, without exception, turned him down. They told Mike to come back in 12 months if he could prove this new model was going to work. 'It was a massive motivator for me, because I'm the kind of person that loves when people think I can't do something because it just puts a fire in my belly,' says Mike. He moved back in with his parents, and put all of his life savings into making Zero Co a reality. He knew that his idea had the potential to hit a nerve with people who shared his vision, and launched a Kickstarter campaign hoping to raise A$250K to get it into production. They raised A$750K, one of the larger Kickstarter success stories of the year, giving him enough runway to get the product made.

Mike brought in three industrial chemists who specialised in making personal-care and cleaning products, and gave them a clear brief of 'essentials' that each formula needed to have. The most important was that the product needed to perform as well as, and ideally better than, the market leaders, 'without any of the nasty ingredients that those products have'.

Every time the chemists developed a formula, it was sent to an independent testing laboratory along with that of their competitors. If the results came back half as effective, they would reformulate over and over until the quality level improved. Mike admits this process was a balancing act of making the products as good as possible while still maintaining their environmental credibility. 'That was the ultimate brief with all of these products,' he says.

Zero Co finally launched in November 2020, and in its first month generated A\$50K of sales, working its way up to A\$1 million a month in sales within ten months, with almost 50,000 households trying it out. Zero Co is kind, impactful, easy and repeatable – and although it's still a relatively new business, it also has the potential to be loved and lasting, if the results of its equity crowdfunding are anything to go by. Using the Birchal platform, Zero Co broke the Australian crowdfunding record by raising the maximum amount allowed by law, A\$5 million, in just a few hours, from 3081 customers who loved the product so much they invested their own money to buy shares in it. That is one of the clearest signs of a killer idea with big potential.

Winners and Losers

Think of creativity as a scale. The point of this book is to show you how to push ideas along the scale from good to great to killer. Killer ideas have many winners in society, the environment or the community. Killer ideas have an almost infinite number of upsides, and few (if any) downsides. They are the results of skilful refinement and tweaking, and tend to tap into wider movements that allow them to spread and have a deeper impact on a wider group of people.

If you were to chart out the differences between the three levels of ideas, it would look like this:

Good Idea	Great Idea	Killer Idea
One party wins	A couple of parties win	Lots of parties win
Some downsides	Some up- and downsides	Lots of upsides
First thoughts	Refined thoughts	Perfecting thoughts
Limited use	Longer use	Unlimited use
Taps into movement	Supported by movement	Starts a movement

Let's now run through an example so it's really clear how to stretch your thinking as much as possible, so you can learn how to do it yourself.

Lots of neighbourhoods have large, boring blank walls, often on the sides of people's houses. In Sydney, most of the inner-city suburbs were developed in the late 1800s and early 1900s, when the former penal colony expanded rapidly and had to house thousands of additional residents as quickly and efficiently as possible. The solution was to build acres of terrace houses, many of them just three to four metres wide, in tight rows where they could squeeze dozens of them together. Walk through the streets of Sydney's Paddington, Darlinghurst and Surry Hills today, and most of the terraces have now been renovated to allow light into their dingy, cramped corners, or had their back walls knocked out to reveal landscaped, urban backyards. At the end of every block of terraces is the corner terrace with a large brick wall the height of the building looming directly over the street, and it's sometimes a little bit ugly.

Let's take that as a starting point for creative thinking: how can you make cities better by doing something with the large, empty walls that exist in every city in the world? We'll use that as a springboard to move along the scale of ideas to see if there's a killer one hiding in there.

So, back to those blank walls of city buildings. What idea can they inspire? What is the first thing that comes to mind?

You will all come up with different ideas at this point, depending on what work you do, who your friends are, what media you consume and where you've travelled to. That's the most wonderful part of creativity: you will rarely get the same idea from everyone. For the sake of this example, one of the first ideas to pop into my head is why don't we paint a mural on the side of the building so it looks better? It's a decent idea, and not that hard to do, depending on which council approves art in your local area. It is not a spectacular one that would make you jealous if you didn't think of it, but it's a good first idea.

Let's evaluate it using a simple test of Winners and Losers:

Winners: Who or what benefits from this?

Losers: Who or what will lose out from this?

Good idea: Paint a mural on the side of a building to make it look better.

Winners:

- People in the neighbourhood will have something nice to look at.
- The artist who paints the mural will get a paid job.
- The owner of the house the mural is painted on might see their property value go up.
- It might prevent vandalism of the blank wall.

Losers:

- People might not like the artwork.
- Neighbours who don't get an artwork on their house.
- The council might get complaints about it.

It's the sort of idea that benefits a few people, but doesn't make a huge impact either way. In other words, it's a good, solid idea.

To turn a good idea into a great one, you need to increase the number of people who benefit from it. The more winners there are for an idea, the better it is. In this example, how can you make more people benefit? One way of doing this is to think further and stretch out the idea behind who the artists are that might feature on the well. If the artists will get paid a commission and additional exposure for their work, are there some types of creatives who would get more benefit from this than others? What if, instead of commissioning just any artist, you only commission up-and-coming or underrepresented artists, who need the exposure. This could help them get their art seen by a lot more people, and the effect you might be able to have on their new careers would be exponentially greater than if you chose well-established artists who already have lots of work around the country. With a small tweak to the idea, it's gone from a good idea to a great one.

Great idea: Use murals on the side of city buildings to profile up-and-coming or underrepresented artists.

Once we apply the same Winners and Losers test to this iteration of the idea, it looks like this.

Winners:

- The people in the neighbourhood will have something nice to look at.
- The value of the house might go up.
- The artist gets a paid job.
- It might prevent vandalism.
- New or underrepresented artists can get their first big break on these murals.
- The communities that surround new and underrepresented artists feel pride in seeing their work on a large scale.

Losers:

- People might not like the artwork.
- Neighbours who don't get an artwork on their house.
- The council might get more complaints about it.

Can you see the difference between a good idea and a great idea now? A good idea is usually the first one you think of that sticks. A great idea is one that's been developed a bit more to stretch out who benefits from it. It takes all the same elements and then leans slightly in a certain direction to make it even better, with even more winners. A great idea is the goal most of the time.

And this brings us to the big, elusive, juicy one: the killer idea. What sets a killer idea apart from every other type of creative idea out there? A killer idea is one that ticks many boxes at the same time. It has a long list of people who benefit from it, and a shorter list of people who don't, if any at all.

If we wanted to turn this example into a really killer idea, you have to think laterally to stretch the idea in many different ways. One way of doing this would be to question why does the artwork need to be on the side of an inner-city building? What would happen if you painted the side of other large objects? And then, stretching a good idea even further, what would happen if you took it outside the city and into another location, like a small regional town?

A killer idea builds and extends on an idea until the winners list is long. A killer idea would be to commission a series of emerging artists to paint football-pitch-sized murals onto the sides of grain silos in regional towns, and then to encourage tourists to visit each location to drive tourism to small towns.

Now that's a killer idea. And the best part? This idea actually exists.[61] In 2015 two street artists were commissioned by FORM, a Western Australian purpose-led art and cultural organisation, to paint eight grain storage bins in the regional farming town of Northam, about 100 kilometres east of Perth. Working from opposite ends of the silos, it took them 16 days and 740 litres of paint to create two contrasting artworks on the massive concrete canvases. The silos attracted visitors from all over to photograph and share them, and began a creative project to transform country infrastructure into sites of world-class mural art. Like any killer idea, it was loved and repeatable, and there are now over 45 painted silos around Australia featuring the work of artists with varying levels of experience. Many of them are linked together to form Silo Art Trails to encourage regional tourism to usually forgotten small towns. A recent survey of 1,100 businesses, residents and visitors to the silo tours by Griffith University found the average visitor spent between $11 and $50 in each location, with some places reaping more benefits than others. In Colbinabbin, a town with a population of 112 that's halfway between Bendigo and Shepparton in central Victoria, six silos painted by artist Tim Bowtell tell the town's history. It draws an estimated 800 people each week, enabling the town's general store to re-open to cater for the crowds.[62]

Using the Winners and Losers evaluation, this stretching of the idea allows a lot more people to benefit.

Killer idea: Create a mural art trail through regional towns to encourage tourism.

Winners:

- The people in the towns will have something nice to look at.
- The owners of the grain silos get great artwork on their properties.
- The artist will get a paid job.
- New or underrepresented artists can get their first big break on these murals.
- The communities that surround new or underrepresented artists, like managers and galleries, get a boost too.
- The towns around the silos will get more visitors.
- Small businesses in the area get additional revenue.
- Accommodation around the silos will be busier.
- Tourism information centres get another product to add to their attractions.
- Car hire companies get more people moving about.
- Local stories and issues can be highlighted through the art.

Losers:

- People might not like the artwork.
- It might cause traffic jams or too much tourism if it gets really popular.

... you can clearly see that the list of winners for this killer idea is already pretty long, with the list of losing parties dwarfed by comparison. The benefits of a killer idea extend into several different communities, in direct and indirect ways.

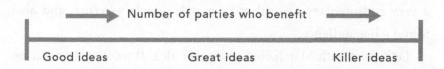

Number of parties who benefit

Good ideas   Great ideas   Killer ideas

Good idea: Paint a mural on the side of a building to make things look better.

Great idea: Use the mural to profile emerging or marginalised artists to help them get a leg-up.

Killer idea: Create a mural art trail through regional towns to encourage tourism.

A good idea becomes a killer idea with the more winning parties it has. It's useful but not always necessary to think of who loses in a situation, so let's look at another real-world example using the same method of stretching out the number of people who benefit. This time we're going online dating.

This story begins all the way back in 1965, when two Harvard students programmed an IBM 1401 computer, about the size of a large office photocopying machine, to create the first computer-based matchmaking service in the United States.[63] A single participant looking for a partner would fill out a 75-question survey, mail it in along with a $3 fee, and wait for a list of matches generated by the computer to come back in the post. It was very successful: over 90,000 people did just that.

That was about the extent of computer-assisted dating until 1995, when the world's first online dating service launched in the United States. Match.com was ahead of its time, taking the accessibility this new thing called the internet offered into millions of people's lives, and allowing anyone to create an online page and look through other people's profiles to try to find someone compatible. It used a very rudimentary algorithm to match people together, and also found a big audience.

Let's start with Match.com as a good idea. If we were to describe what sites like Match, as well as RSVP, eHarmony, Plenty of Fish and others did in a single phrase, it would be something like this: they create online profiles you can search through to find a compatible partner.

Running through who the 'Winners' would be from the ideal of online dating, you might come up with this.

Good idea: Creating online profiles to find someone compatible to date.

Winners:

- **People who save time dating:** Instead of people having to leave their homes and hope serendipity plays a part, online dating made the entire process a lot more convenient. You could browse hundreds of people's profiles in a few hours, a process that in the real world might take you years to actually do (if you could even meet hundreds of single people at once). You could now know if someone likes death-metal music or long walks on the beach at sunset before you'd even had your first drink.

- **Couples with increased diversity:** It was no longer just the people you bumped into down at the coffee shop in your dating pool: it was now people who lived on the other side of town, or even in different states from you. Interestingly, research from the National Academy of Sciences has shown that after the launch of Match.com in 1995, interracial marriages in the US began to increase.[64] This can't be solely attributed to online dating, but the benefits of increasing the diversity of your potential partners in all aspects can't be understated.

- **Introverts:** Instead of having to walk up to someone in a bar and put yourself out there, when you date online you only need to click a few buttons. It removes some of the fear of rejection that traditionally weighs heavily in real-life interactions.

- **Online dating companies:** There's no denying that the companies that got in early and dominated the first wave of dating on the internet, like Match.com, eHarmony and RSVP, did very well as consumers parted with serious amounts of money to meet people in a more convenient way.

There are other parties who have benefited from the rise of online dating, but they are the main winners. If we were going to start listing out every single party that 'lost' from computer-assisted dating, we could also write a list just as long (or, some would argue, even longer!). But for the sake of this exercise, we're going to stick with the winners only.

Online dating using a desktop computer was a good idea, arguably a very good idea, and it has survived, in various different forms, for over 20 years. But how can you make it better?

That's a question a bunch of 20-year-olds tried to answer in 2012 when they saw that the proliferation of smartphones was rapidly changing industries around them. During a 'hackathon' to play around with rapidly developing tech products, the general manager of Hatch Labs, Sean Rad, worked with Joe Munoz to create a prototype for a mobile dating app that would become the basis of Tinder. Originally called MatchBox, it took some of the original idea behind Match.com and tweaked it for a new audience and new technologies.[65] The app would only exist on mobile phones and added the gamification of swiping to see potential matches, which made the whole experience feel a lot fresher. Tinder was a great idea, and it took off almost immediately in college towns around the US. Within two years of launching, it processed more than a billion swipes left and right every single day.

Of course, there are positives and negatives to the gamification of meeting people, but I can weirdly say I'm one of the app's success stories. I met my husband on Tinder in 2014, each of us swiping right on the other's profile back when mobile dating felt fun and new. It still took the serendipity of us colliding in our local cafe and awkwardly recognising each other from Tinder until we decided to go on our first date, but if it wasn't for the invention of this dating app we would most likely still be strangers in a cafe.

That's just one of the reasons mobile dating apps like Tinder were a great idea. They took the original concept of meeting people using computers, and refined it based on location and friendship circles.

So who were the winners when Tinder first launched? It was built on the back of another online dating platform, which means that a lot of original winners were still there.

Great idea: Use mobile phones to match people who might like each other.

Winners:

All of the same parties who came out ahead with the previous iteration of the idea are the same, with the addition of:

- **Even more people:** Even more consumers tried online dating for the first time thanks to apps like Tinder because they helped decrease the social stigma around it, as well as reducing the friction required to sign up. You can download and be swiping in just a few minutes thanks to profiles coming across from other social media sites.
- **Mobile phone companies:** Apps like Tinder are, let's face it, addictive. They are so sticky that in 2014 the *New York*

Times reported that people were logging in to the app 11 times a day.[67] Whether we liked that or not, it makes our phones even harder to part with.

- **Consumers' egos got a boost:** There is something very appealing about the instant gratification that comes from matching with a stranger on Tinder. Sure, it's not exactly healthy in the long term, but getting small ego boosts has played a large part in Tinder's success.

- **Fewer rejected daters:** On Tinder you can only message if both parties swipe right to say they like each other. This removes some of the fear of rejection, which means the people you end up chatting with already like each other in some way.

You can already see how an idea is moved along the scale from a good idea to a great one by twisting the idea until it benefits more parties. So, how can you take an idea like Tinder and make it better just by tweaking it some more?

That's exactly what Whitney Wolfe Herd was thinking when she decided to improve on mobile dating apps. Whitney was one of the co-founders of Tinder, joining the original team a few months in, marketing and spearheading their efforts to recruit colleges onto the platform. Their marketing was successful, but Whitney broke off a personal relationship with one of the other co-founders and left the company.

Whitney was very familiar with the platform, and all the problems that arose when traditional power dynamics were imposed on people's interactions within it. One flaw in Tinder's set-up was that it allowed men to harass women in messages. Whitney decided to launch a new dating app to invert the dynamic by giving only women the power to initiate conversations, and not men. It was a simple extension of Tinder's idea, but it had a huge effect. Whitney's dating app, Bumble, launched in 2014, and that tweak – putting the safety of women first – helped turn Bumble into a killer idea.

Whitney told *Marie Claire* that the secret to innovation was fixing things: 'Look at what is broken in society, figure out how to make it better, and then, around that, formulate a business,' she said.[68] 'That's how we get all our ideas. Like, "Wow! I wish that existed in real life"… And then a year later, it's the number-one thing in the App Store.'

Bumble now boasts over 50 million users and US$500million in annual revenue. When it listed on the US stock exchange, it made Whitney the world's youngest self-made billionaire, and the youngest woman to take a tech unicorn public, valuing the entire company at US$13 billion.[69]

Killer idea: Mobile dating app that empowers women to make the first move.

If you were to list out who wins with Bumble, it would basically be the same parties as Tinder, with the addition of…

Winners:

- **Women looking for dates:** The interface tweak means women are empowered to make the first move in new relationships if they want to. If they don't, then it's also up to them. It's a small difference with a big impact.

- **People who want to find new friends:** The success of Bumble led to a new app called Bumble BFF that matches you with friends of the same gender to take some of the awkwardness out of making new friends.

- **Networkers:** Due to its popularity, another side of the Bumble app, Bumble Bizz, allows you to put your work and profession at the forefront and meet other people in similar industries to you for networking opportunities.

While the dating side of Bumble is its biggest attraction, once you've got an audience of millions of people it's easy to stretch it out to even more. That's what Bumble has consciously done, continually adding new parties who stand to benefit from their killer idea.

These are two examples of ideas that have been stretched to go from good to great to killer. Once you've got the germ of an idea, that is all you need to start moving it along the scale until there are lots of parties who are going to benefit.

IRL

Step 6: Stretch It Out

Good ideas can always be better, and thinking about them on a scale of who benefits is a way of helping that process along. If you want to use killer thinking in your work and life, this is how to do it.

Exercise 11: Winners and Losers

The model we've demonstrated in this step can be easily applied to any idea you want to stretch and improve.

1. Create two columns, marked 'Winners' and 'Losers'.
It should look like this:

Idea:	
Winners	**Losers**

2. Write a list of everyone who will benefit from your idea in the 'Winners' column.
Try to make it as comprehensive and thorough as you can. Some prompts to help you capture this:

- Who directly 'wins' from it?
- Which parties indirectly benefit?
- What are the positives for society because of this idea?
- Who makes money from this?
- What are the benefits besides monetary return?
- If your idea didn't exist, who would miss it?
- Are there any additional communities who get something from it?

3. Write out who won't benefit from your idea in the 'Losers' column.

If your idea came to life, who would potentially not benefit from it? Some prompts for this:

- What are the potential negative repercussions of this idea?
- Who would not like it?
- Would there be any complaints about it?
- Would anyone lose money if it were successful?
- Who is the 'competition' for this idea?

4. Think of how you can increase the 'Winners'.

Once you've drawn up your tables, do you have more parties in the 'Winners' or 'Losers' column? If the number of people and communities who would benefit outweighs the other column, then your idea has some serious potential.

It's then time to think about how you can refine your idea so more people benefit from it. Are there any parties in the 'Losers' column who could actually become 'Winners' with some small tweaks to your idea? The aim is to have as few parties as possible in the 'Losers' column.

5. Create a 'Winners and Losers' list for every idea you have.
Repeat the steps above for every idea that's on your shortlist, and you should quickly get a sense of which idea has the most ability to have an impact on the world. This simple exercise will highlight which ideas are good, which ones are great, and – the holy grail of ideas – which are truly killer ones you need to start thinking about implementing at the right moment.

Fast Takeaways

1. Think of creativity as a scale; your job is to move ideas from good to great to killer along it.
2. A good idea is usually the first one you think of, and it should be used as a baseline to be improved and modified.
3. In a good idea usually just one party wins; great ideas have a few winners; and killer ideas share the wins around many different people and communities.
4. The best ideas are tested and tweaked as they go.
5. To make an idea better, ask who or what benefits from this and refine it so that more people benefit.

Step 7:
Launch into a Rising Tide

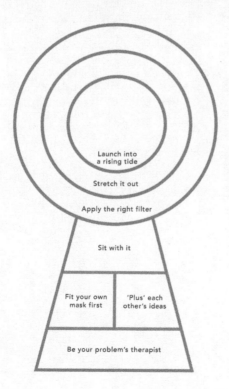

Launch into
a rising tide

Stretch it out

Apply the right filter

Sit with it

Fit your own
mask first

'Plus' each
other's ideas

Be your problem's therapist

Nothing is more powerful than an idea whose time has come.

Victor Hugo, poet and novelist

Launch into a Rising Tide

The 1960s in America was a wild time in history. Major political events dominated the decade, from the Vietnam War to the Cuban Missile Crisis, the assassinations of John F Kennedy and Martin Luther King to the growing civil rights and women's liberation movements. It was a heady time for a superpower grappling with its postwar influence in a rapidly changing world.

A young, idealistic student, Jaime Ortiz Mariño, found himself at the centre of this when he moved from Bogotá in Colombia to Case Western Reserve University in Ohio in 1967 to study architecture. 'I faced a reality of the United States that wasn't my image of it,' says Jaime now, over half a century later. 'The society was in turmoil, and I was very impressed with how a counterculture was being created out of the streets.'

There was energy everywhere Jaime looked in America: students protesting against the long-running Vietnam War, a growing environmental consciousness that would evolve into the hippie movement of the 1970s, and the second wave of feminism that an empowered generation was fighting for. All of these movements were rising at the same time, creating an electrifying moment in history.

When Jaime moved back Bogotá he noticed that urbanisation was in full swing there. In the 1950s, 75 per cent of Colombia's population lived in rural areas, and the shift of many of these Colombians to urban centres was creating a steady drumbeat of migration that has led now to three quarters of the population living in cities today. In many discussions with his friend, and fellow architect, Fernando Caro Restrepo, they could both see echoes of the United States' urbanisation in Colombia, a society where cars ruled the streets, with little room for any other forms of transport.

Jaime and Fernando could sense this movement, and wanted to ensure that the humble bicycle would still have a place in the future cities. 'I wanted to place the bicycle at the forefront of the political and social debate,' says Jaime. Together with some friends, they identified a problem: Why should cars be the sole occupants of roads? What about pedestrians, bikes and families?

Jaime thought a lot about the design of Colombian cities, where every town has a plaza at the heart of it. The plaza is a perfect example of the concept of a temporary use of a space. It was conceived with changing audiences and needs at its heart. In the morning, it is a market. Later it becomes an avenue to go to church, or for local politicians to canvass. At the end of each day, people gather to drink, socialise or just wander the plaza and meet other people. It has multiple uses depending on the time and day of the week.

So, thought Jaime, why not apply this same principle to the roads that were increasingly taking up more and more space in an increasingly urbanised society? They came up with an idea: to close down city streets for a period of time and open them up only to bikes and walkers. They took their idea to the city administration and, surprisingly, the administration agreed to shut down some of the streets in central Bogotá to see what would happen.

The first event was held on 14 December 1974. Six thousand people turned up to explore the streets without cars: enough of a success for them to repeat the experiment about a year later on 12 October, with some tweaks. This time, the mayor wanted to understand its effect and commissioned a study to show its positive impact.

The following year, in June 1976, the city legislated to turn their idea into an official public event, and the modern version of La Ciclovía was born. Today, from seven am to two pm every Sunday, 120 kilometres of streets are shut down for Ciclovía, and the streets of Bogotá are turned over to the people. Every weekend two million people – just under a third of the city's population – come out of their houses to enjoy the streets without any cars. It's one of the most successful civic programs in the world, and it all started with a killer idea from Jaime and his friends.

There are over 400 cities around the world that now run a version of Ciclovía, from Paris to Philadelphia, with benefits across lots of parts of society. 'Ciclovía is a people's event,' says Jaime. 'Anyone who goes out on the street feels like a main actor. There are no second-class actors in Ciclovía. We are all first-class actors... it's a landmark in our city.'

Part of its appeal, and the reason it has been able to spread far throughout the world despite language and cultural difficulties, lies in its ability for anyone to be involved. 'It's something that doesn't require money or a big political movement,' says Jaime. 'It's something you can do in front of your house. As simple as it is, it's so well rooted as an event created by people for people.'

La Ciclovía hitched itself onto the back of the trend of growing urbanisation. As people migrated to the city, they needed to feel connected with each other and with their environment. It's a powerful movement that's fuelled the staying power of La Ciclovía for almost 50 years, and will continue to power it for the next 50.

Pick Your Moment

There are some movements you can sense are building around you. Jaime Ortiz Mariño and his friends felt a movement around them, and came up with the idea at the right moment in history. Would it have been as successful if it had launched a decade earlier? There's no definite answer, but I doubt it would have been as lasting if it hadn't ridden on the coattails of a larger cultural movement.

We're living in a time when there are movements all around us. From the green tidal wave of environmentalism to the long-overdue march of equality, at any given moment there are multiple movements that you can hook your idea into to give it its best chance of thriving. If you can launch your idea on a tide that's already rising, then half the work of getting people excited about your idea will already be done by the power of the movement. Of course, this can't be done in an inauthentic way or it just won't work. You can't add your idea onto a movement unless it is a meaningful contributor to it.

Sometimes an idea needs to bide its time until it's the right moment to launch it. If you catch the right cultural force, there's a chance your killer idea can be long lasting and repeatable.

So what are the rising tides at the moment? Here are some of the most powerful global movements that will be defining how we live and work for decades to come.

Sustainability

The growing awareness of our effect on the world around us is not a trend that's going to go away. The rise of the 'conscious consumer' over the past few decades has been well documented, and a majority of people believe the power of business can be used to enact real change in this area as it becomes only more important over the coming years. 'Climate change is the next major mega-trend, and we believe it represents the biggest investment opportunity since the internet,' said portfolio manager at Munro Partners James Tsinidis.[70] 'We're just at the beginning of the next big S-curve, a massive and sustainable decades-long growth trend.'

Temporary Use of Space

With a growing population, our spaces are becoming more crowded and rare. Proponents of this movement believe physical spaces can serve multiple needs at different times, like a shop that hosts a co-working space during the day, and diners by night. Mixed-use spaces can increase the convenience, utility and profitability of a space.

Sharing Economy

There are so many things we use that we no longer need to own. From cars to clothes to houses, the more we share items with others, the less need for waste in the world. The shift from owning to hiring is full of opportunities.

Holistic Wellness

We are becoming more aware of the need to be well in all aspects of our lives, prompting the rise of everything from meditation and mindfulness practices to an increase in alternatives to alcoholic and sugary drinks and food.

Empowerment

For too long the rights of minorities and those with less power in our community have been denied. Finally, after centuries of struggle, the fight for equality is now too big for the mainstream to ignore. There are countless powerful movements, from Black Lives Matter to #MeToo, which are giving much-needed space to ideas that highlight empowerment in all of its forms.

Decentralisation

We're right at the start of a moment that's transferring historical ideas of control and decision-making from key individuals, businesses and governments to a distributed network. Blockchain technology, for example, with its potential to democratise power out of the hands of a few and into the hands of many, will create so many opportunities for fresh thinking.

Circular Economy

There is a real drive to reuse, repair and recycle goods so that materials and resources can be better used to get more value out of them. Many businesses are now creating cycles that value a user, rather than just a consumer.

Plant-Based Future

Health has always been important, but there's an increasing trend for consumers to focus on this themselves, with many reassessing what they eat and the impact it has. Plant-based food sales have skyrocketed in most Western countries over the last few years, and this increase will only continue as improved taste and technology catches up.

Online Everything

The coronavirus pandemic fast-forwarded an entire decade's worth of trends in just a few months. McKinsey reported that during the first few months of the Covid-19 pandemic three quarters of US consumers tried different stores, websites or brands they had never bought from before, and almost two thirds of them expect to keep using them once things start getting a bit back to normal.[71] If there was ever a time to launch something new or ramp up your marketing to find a new audience off the back of a global wave of opportunity, then this is it.

*

These are just a taste of the massive societal trends building momentum right now, but every industry and location will have its own micro trends. Look around you and observe where people's attention is going, and you'll soon be able to sense where to focus your killer thinking.

Ben Liebmann has spent most of his life working in the space between art and commerce, most recently as the Chief Operating Officer at Noma, the ground-breaking restaurant helmed by chef René Redzepi that's been named the world's best five times over and spawned a culinary revolution that's redefined Nordic food.

Ben jokingly calls himself 'a suit amongst creatives' and has worked with musicians, songwriters, television producers and chefs to bring to life their ideas with unparalleled success. 'I take no credit for what takes place within the four walls of the restaurant,' explains Ben from Copenhagen. 'The chefs and the front-of-house team create something that is truly extraordinary. What I do is help them build a business that wraps around that.'

Ben has surfed many rising tides of movements over the years, beginning his career in the music industry just as digital technology upended how we bought and listened to music. He clearly remembers sitting in an office in Sydney's Crows Nest in the early 2000s looking at a report about a little-known audio streaming service called Napster that allowed people to share digital files with each other. The bewildered record company executives were obsessed with a tiny number in the bottom of the screen that showed how many people were sharing files with each other at any given time. To them, every number represented a lost single or album sale, but Ben saw opportunity. 'Those people wanted our product,' he recalls, 'but just not in the way that we gave it to them. So how do we deliver that content in a different way?' It would take the music industry two decades to answer that question by making streaming music in apps like Spotify easier than stealing it.

One of Ben's favourite sayings is a line he picked up from an old boss: 'Push the bruises.' It means that it's important to find the pain points in any model or situation, and intentionally explore them to get to the core of a problem quicker. 'It's our place to push the bruises to ask, "Does this fit within the values that the creatives have built the business around?" And if it doesn't, then it's our responsibility to help make that happen.'

But Ben didn't have time to wait, as he saw another rising tide in the world of entertainment, where commerce and content were smashing into each other in lots of ways. Ben became the Global CEO of Shine 360°, the rights management division of Shine Group, an entertainment company started by Elisabeth Murdoch. Shine 360° took television shows like *MasterChef* (broadcast in 110 countries) and created a dizzying array of brand extensions like magazines, books, cookware and events that generated hundreds of millions of dollars of revenue. For two decades Ben has specialised in taking the creative seeds of an idea, then building a sustainable business around it – and giving it the best chance of success by picking the right time to launch.

Sell Your Idea In

If I asked you what was the most watched scripted limited series on Netflix to date, you probably wouldn't guess it is a show about chess. *The Queen's Gambit*, released in October 2020, saw 62 million accounts around the world watching it in its first 28 days, the most ever at the time.[72] It made the Top 10 shows in 92 countries, and number one in 63 countries. It might seem like an overnight success, but it took nine rewrites and 30 years of perseverance to get there.

The Queen's Gambit was originally a novel written in 1983 by American writer Walter Tevis. It follows the fictional life of an orphaned female chess prodigy, Beth Harmon, who overcomes adversity in the 1950s to reach the highest levels of chess. After falling in love with the book, the chairman of Scottish whisky company Macallan-Glenlivet, who writes under the name Allan Scott, purchased an option to bring the book to life as a television series in 1989. A few years later, he paid an even larger sum to buy the rights to turn it into a movie. The rights needed to be renewed every year, and Allan paid the fee consistently in a sign of his faith in the idea.

As well as running the whisky company, Allan is a very accomplished writer, writing the screenplay for *Castaway* with Tom Hanks, and the 1990 movie adaptation of Roald Dahl's *The Witches*, among others. Despite his success, every studio he took *The Queen's Gambit* to for decades turned him down. Various directors were attached to make versions of it, from Italian director Bernardo Bertolucci, the man responsible for such classics as *Last Tango in Paris* and *The Last Emperor*, to Australian actor Heath Ledger, who was on board to direct a movie version before his death in 2008.

Finally, after 30 years of renewing the rights, and nine separate rewrites of the material, Scott teamed up with Scott Frank, who wrote the screenplays for *Minority Report* and *Logan*, and turned the story into a limited release series for Netflix. It would have been easy for Scott to give up any time over the decades, but he didn't. Instead, he doubled down every year, confident that the content would eventually find its home and audience. Even after it was turned down by studio after studio, who told him the subject matter was too dull to ever take off, he refined his pitch and continued to try to sell it.

To get your idea off the ground at the right time, you have to communicate and sell it to other people. Famed creative founder David Ogilvy wrote that 'in the modern world of business, it is useless to be a creative original thinker unless you can also sell what you create. Management cannot be expected to recognise a good idea unless it is presented to them by a good salesman.'[73]

I started my career as a music journalist writing 50-word album reviews, and quickly realised it's easier to write 500 words than it is to cut and edit until there is not one wasted word. I've seen hundreds of documents where competing ideas are all thrown on top of each other until the result is a mess. Thankfully, knowing how to clarify your thoughts is a skill you can develop.

It's something that a lot of people struggle with, even globally praised film directors like Quentin Tarantino. One year at the Sundance Film Festival, the *Pulp Fiction* director was having lunch with fellow creative Terry Gilliam and was in a bit of a bind. 'I said, "You have a very specific vision in your movies, it's right there on the screen. How do you do that? How do you get that vision that's in your head onto the screen?"' recalled Tarantino many years later.[74] Gilliam, a former member of the Monty Python comedy troupe, responded that as a director that's not his job. 'Your job is to hire talented people who can do that. You hire a cinematographer who can get the kind of quality that you want. You don't have to know how to pick up and take the lights around to create an effect. You hire a costume designer who can give the colours that you need and the flamboyance, or not, that you require. You hire a production designer who can do that. Your job is explaining your vision. Your job is articulating to them what you want on the screen.' Tarantino describes that moment as pivotal for him in understanding his craft. As a creative, what he needed to do was be super clear in communicating his vision to everyone around him so they could help execute it.

It's the same with any idea. You need to be able to clearly and succinctly describe your idea, every minute of every day, to your audience, to clients, colleagues, the council, to your bank, your mum and investors. That is where the art of simplification comes in. With every project, simplify it until you can describe it in just one page, then one paragraph and finally in just one sentence.

The idea on a page: Explain what your idea is, why it's needed and how it works. A whole page is too much blank space for our purposes, but you should start with this to get it all out of your head.

The idea in a paragraph: Now look at the page full of words, and try to cut it down to just a single paragraph. How can you communicate what it's about in just a few sentences? This is hard but forces you to cut though the noise.

The idea in a sentence: How can you succinctly summarise your idea in a single sentence? Try to make it jargon-free and something even a child would understand.

In the IRL section at the end of this chapter there are exercises to help you clearly summarise your idea so others can get just as excited about it as you are.

A similar concept applies to television shows and movies, where entire series can be sold or cancelled based on these one-line precis. In the entertainment world they call it a logline, a throwback to a time in old Hollywood when big studios who bought lots of scripts would keep a 'log book' that contained a one-line, concise summary that described every movie they owned. Loglines are now serious business, and are sometimes the difference between a show or film being commissioned or not. If you can't sum it up in a simple sentence, then how is a viewer going to explain the show to their partner as they're sitting on the couch trying to think of what to watch next?

Some of the most iconic and successful TV shows in history are instantly recognisable just by their loglines.

A 17-year-old aristocrat falls in love with a kind but poor artist aboard the luxurious, ill-fated RMS Titanic.

A pragmatic palaeontologist visiting an almost complete theme park is tasked with protecting a couple of kids after a power failure causes the park's cloned dinosaurs to run loose.

A mockumentary on a group of typical office workers, where the workday consists of ego clashes, inappropriate behaviour and tedium.

If you correctly guessed *Titanic*, *Jurassic Park* and *The Office* then you can already see the power in making something super easy to understand in one succinct sentence.

You don't have to do it alone either: it's not only up to you to help bring ideas to life. Murray Bell is the founder of Semi Permanent, a company that connects creative talent, brands and audiences together. Their namesake brand and design festival has been held in Sydney, Auckland, Singapore, Abu Dhabi and Portugal since 2002, with speakers like filmmakers Oliver Stone and Michel Gondry, and artists like Banksy and Shepard Fairy.

Murray has worked with some of the most creative minds in the world, and has noticed a common factor in their overwhelming success. Part of it can be attributed to their ability to share their vision with trusted people who help them execute it. 'The top-tier people that I know creatively always have a killer 2IC [second-in-charge],' says Murray. 'Someone right next to them who is very comfortable with being completely anonymous... a lot of the designers have people around them that are very good. That gives them the ability to free themselves a little bit from the commercial.'

Murray references the late Off-White founder and CEO Virgil Abloh, and artists like Daniel Arsham, CJ Hendry and Scott Dadich as people he's worked with who all have close partners who help them bring their large creative visions to life. 'The 2IC is someone that can decipher the code of that person,' he says. 'The reality is you only have a short amount of time, and I think that's probably what some of these great creatives realise. They have good ideas, and ideas come around pretty often. But it's actually the converting on those things, and you just can't get them done on your own.'

It's important to know your strengths and surround yourself with people who complement your weaknesses. Lisa Messenger, the founder of Collective Hub, has written over 40 books and now knows exactly what she is – and isn't – good at. 'I have a hundred ideas before breakfast!' she says. 'Ideas aren't the problem for me, execution and implementation are... I have to have very detail-orientated implementers around me or nothing would ever happen.' Lisa creates the initial spark, then checks in with her team to flesh her ideas out and create a simple financial model to ensure they're viable. Remo Giuffré, the founder of TEDxSydney and creative strategist, spends a lot of time ensuring everyone around him knows the 'why' behind what they're doing. 'Clarity of vision is critical,' he says. 'And it's not good enough to just have the vision, you need to be able to communicate and inspire people around you. It's always better when people understand why they're doing what they're doing, and ideally why those reasons are worthwhile.' If you can refine and clarify your creative idea so that everyone can understand it easily and help bring it to life, you're well on your way to getting other people to see your vision and enabling them to share it further.

Ride the Movement

When Abigail Forsyth and her brother Jamie started a chain of cafes in Melbourne in the late 1990s, the environment was not on their mind. They just wanted to make great coffee and healthy food as well as they could. Over the next few years, they grew the business and started noticing how many disposable coffee cups they were going through. The cups were lined with polyethylene, a synthetic resin that's one of the most widely produced plastics in the world, which meant they couldn't be recycled. Thinking about thousands of coffee cups being discarded from their cafes alone each week led Abigail and Jamie to explore their own killer idea: customers should be able to keep their own coffee cup and use it again.

They had been running the cafes for a decade by then before the idea properly developed, and in 2008 they designed their prototype of the first barista-standard reusable coffee cup and sold it at markets. One day alone they sold more than 1000 of their KeepCups at a Melbourne design market stall and realised they were onto something. In 2010 they launched a London office, followed a few years later with another in LA. Today, KeepCup has grown to define an entire product category, having sold more than ten million reusable cups in more than 75 countries around the world and allowing customers to divert millions of disposable cups from landfill every day.

Abigail attributes some of their success to having launched the idea at the right time. For decades, people who cared about the environment were classified as extreme 'greenies' who didn't represent the mainstream, but by 2010 that was shifting alongside a growing realisation that human actions were having large and devastating effects on our world. 'The broadening out of the sustainability conversation and being at the helm of that discourse was really important,' recalls Abigail. 'At the time KeepCup was starting to take shape, there were the "greenies" and then there was everyone else. We felt strongly that you didn't have to be a greenie to want to do the right thing by the environment. We believed that there were other ways to draw people into the conversation on sustainability and waste reduction.'

KeepCup hit a nerve. People were looking for tangible ways they could increase sustainability in their own lives. The newly launched reusable KeepCups gave consumers an accessible way to change their habits. 'We were connecting to some larger ideas about what a good life looks like, about what consuming coffee looks like. We asked ourselves a simple question – how do we achieve this in a way that's both beautiful and enjoyable? Making sure we don't forget about the simple pleasure of drinking coffee and the quality of the experience, I think, is another reason why the product has been so successful.'

Julia Kay from Great Wrap admires the way that KeepCup were able to launch successfully into the rising tide at a time when not many others could see the opportunity. 'You've got to admire the early KeepCup work,' she says, 'because that was a real cultural shift… you're making people change their deeply engrained habit.'

As well as launching a product, they created a new category, with KeepCup now basically the generic word to describe any coffee mug that gets reused, but it's an idea that's been refined a lot along the way. 'People who come into work at KeepCup often say, "I thought it was just a cup. I didn't realise how much thought has gone into the product." That attention to detail, the understanding of how a coffee cup is used behind the machine, how it's used in front of the machine, all the time spent on product design, trialling and refinement, allowed us to stand the test of time.' The original KeepCups were made from plastic before they switched to predominantly glass, and they are constantly trying to think of new ways to fulfil their original aim. 'One of the things that sets us apart is that we started by trying to solve an environmental problem. This urged us to view everything through the lens of longevity of product use,' says Abigail. 'The most important thing is that people take our product, enjoy it and use it. Every. Single. Day. This is what makes it all worthwhile.'

KeepCup is a killer idea that's kind, impactful, loved, lasting, easy and repeatable. It owes some of its success to the growing environmental movement it's been able to ride all the way to becoming a household name.

IRL

Step 7: Launch into a Rising Tide

The right idea at the right time is very powerful. By following global trends and building ideas that fit into their slipstream, you'll give your idea the best chance of really taking off. You also need to be able to sell your creativity as succinctly as you can so that others can do your job for you. This is how.

Exercise 12: Rising Tides

Every industry is unique, and the trends that are rising and falling in the area in which you want to launch an idea are dependent on your location, when you're reading this, and what you want to achieve. However, this exercise will show you how to start exploring some of the rising tides that are all around you.

1. Go to trends.google.com in your browser.
Google Trends is a free and underused resource that analyses the popularity of the top search queries around the world, and presents them in simple graphs so you can see what is trending over time.

The data allows you to search by your location, and whatever time period you want. I suggest starting with global trends before narrowing it down to your country, and looking at the last one to five years to give a good snapshot.

2. Type in a topic that you want to search for.
Type in the area you're thinking of launching an idea into. Google Trends will tell you if the volume of search queries is increasing, decreasing or staying the same. You can change the locations and time range to view trends in all different combinations – it's an extremely valuable free tool.

3. Explore topics that have recently trended.

If you don't have a particular area you want to know about and just wish to be inspired, the beauty of Google Trends is that it shows you what topics have recently been trending, as well as what has historically been searched in each country by year. For example, if you were following Google Trends in 2013 you would see that one of the top searches of the year was 'Bitcoin', when the price of one Bitcoin was just US$13. It gives a glimpse of how cryptocurrencies would grow in prominence, and value, over the next few years.

4. Use data to know when to launch.

The data doesn't lie, and if interest is really dying down in your area it's probably a sign that the tide is receding, but if the graph is trending upwards it's probably a good time to launch. Combine this research with your own to help you determine whether you're going to give your idea the best possible chance of succeeding.

Exercise 13: Idea in a Sentence

One of the most important things you can do is learn to succinctly communicate your idea to other people. Having a clear, easy-to-pass-on sentence will become your most powerful marketing tool to help launch your idea into the world, so every word should be perfected. To create the sentence for your idea, you need to start with more words and edit it down.

1. Write about your idea in a single page.

Sometimes even summarising an idea onto a single page can be difficult. What to leave out and what to include? You want your summary to be an explainer that clearly describes what your idea is as though you're telling someone who has never heard of it before.

You might have to write pages of information before editing it down to one page, but a good place to start is the Five Ws: who, what, where, when and why. If you're having trouble knowing where to start, begin with each of these as a guide to writing your idea down on one single page.

Who: Who is the target market for your idea?
What: What is your idea all about?
Where: In what location will your idea take place?
When: How soon will the idea launch?
Why: What are the main reasons your idea will work?

If you need to, you can also add 'How' as the final prompter to get you writing about your idea. How will the idea come to life?

Start writing to answer each question and before you know it, you should have a page full of words. Once you've written each of the Five Ws, move the text around the page so you begin with the most important information first. Edit the words until you have a simple one-pager on exactly what your idea is.

2. Write about your idea in a single paragraph.

Now you've got a full page of writing about your idea, you need to edit it down into just one paragraph of information. If you've already ordered your full page with the most important info at the start, then use that as a base and add in only the parts of other paragraphs that are absolutely essential. Cut down any unnecessary words (this is hard! I know!), and keep editing and throwing out anything that's not needed. At the end, you should have a single paragraph that sums up your idea.

3. Write about your idea in a single sentence.

Think of this as your elevator pitch. If you had just a few seconds in an elevator to explain your idea to someone, what would you say? Observe how you communicate your idea to someone for the first time. Is there a clear way of saying it? What sentence do people react to the most?

There are three keys to cutting your single paragraph down into just one simple sentence:

- take out any words or concepts that are repetitive;
- clarify anything an eight-year-old wouldn't understand; and
- edit out unnecessary words with confidence.

Don't worry about cutting things out. In fact, you should cut it down as much as possible. Cut out anything that's not needed right now. Be brutal. The best ideas are expressed in single sentences so they can be repeated by others.

Fast Takeaways

1. If you can launch your idea into a cultural or social movement that's already rising, then half the work of getting people excited about your idea will already be done.
2. Current movements include sustainability, the temporary use of space, empowerment, decentralisation, the sharing and circular economies, plant-based food and the shift to online everything.
3. You need to be able to clearly and succinctly describe your idea, every minute of every day, to everyone around it.
4. Simplify what you do into a single sentence (it's harder than you think).
5. Build a team around you who you trust to communicate, and execute, your vision.

Step 8:
Listen with Open Ears

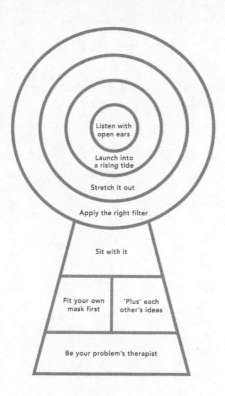

Listen with
open ears

Launch into
a rising tide

Stretch it out

Apply the right filter

Sit with it

Fit your own
mask first

'Plus' each
other's ideas

Be your problem's therapist

There's a lot of
difference between
listening and hearing.

GK Chesterton, writer

Listen with Open Ears

One of the world's most successful products has sold over 100 billion units, but it almost didn't turn out that way. It all began in the 1880s when an American lawyer, John Loud, searched for a way to write on rough materials like leather and wood just as easily as paper. At that time, fountain pens were the only solution, using a wet, inky solution that was temperamental at best. John tried various options, eventually settling on the genius idea of using a tiny steel ball held in place by a socket. He filed a patent in 1888. 'My invention,' he wrote in the filing,[75] 'is especially useful, among other purposes, for marking on rough surfaces – such as wood, coarse wrapping-paper, and other articles where an ordinary pen could not be used.'

But unfortunately for John, that was about the extent of it. Every time it was used on paper, the rough pen tore right through the delicate material. No one bought his basically useless pen and it was deemed a commercial failure. Eventually the patent for the world's first ballpoint pen just lapsed and joined the millions of failed inventions that never found their audience.

Half a decade later, the problems with fountain pens still existed, frustrating and annoying every user who stained their hands and smudged their pages with the messy ink. One of those people was a young Hungarian journalist, László Bíró, who knew there had to be a better solution. He knew of John Loud's invention, and spent time thinking about everything that was wrong with it, in particular the main problem: the type of ink traditionally used in fountain pens didn't work well in the ballpoint.

Creativity is all about connecting ideas, and László saw that the newspaper ink he was familiar with was thicker and quicker-drying than the usual pen ink. He realised if he could adapt this for the ballpoint, he'd invent a better pen. László tasked his brother, György, who was a dentist by trade and knew all about chemistry, with devising a new formula for a more efficient ink that spread easily and dried quickly.

László took the key principles behind the ballpoint pen – a tiny bearing that gets drenched in ink on one side and trails it out the other using gravity – and perfected it, adding things like a tiny hole in the barrel's body that keeps the air pressure inside and outside equal so it flows easily.

He filed a patent for his pen in Britain in 1938, just before World War II forced the brothers to flee Hungary for Argentina, where they continued to work on their invention every moment they could. In 1943, while the war was still raging, they released their pen, called the 'birome'. The birome allowed people to write in any situation, and one of their first large orders came from the British Royal Air Force, which bought 30,000 pens so their pilots could use them while flying.

Over the next decade, several companies would compete with their own versions of the ballpoint pens in different countries, most of them high-end expensive products that cost about the same amount as a secretary's average weekly wage.[76] It took a Frenchman, Marcel Bich, to really see its full potential. The 1950s saw the rising tide of easily accessible, low-cost plastic production and he bought a factory on the outskirts of Paris that he re-tooled so it could produce his own, better version using László's designs.

Bich's version of the ballpoint pen was dramatically cheaper than any other on the market, making it accessible for the first time by anyone. An advertising guru persuaded Bich to shorten his family's name on the pen to the globally instantly understood Bic, and the 'Bic Biro' – officially known as the Bic Cristal Ballpoint Pen – went on to revolutionise handwriting around the world and sell enough pens to draw a line to the moon and back more than 320,000 times.[77]

The journey to one of the world's bestselling products was anything but straightforward, zigzagging over decades of invention and re-invention, heading down dead ends, and continually being tweaked as technology and consumers' needs caught up to it. At every stage the various businesspeople working on the idea had to listen to feedback, change their strategy and adapt it to get the Biro where it is today: a product that, literally, rewrote history.

Coming up with ideas is the easy part, and working through all the obstacles to getting it as good in real life as it is in your head is, well, bloody hard. There's no sense mincing words here. Some people tend to freeze right in this process, content to constantly think up new ideas and file them away into the 'someday maybe' folder in their brain. Others can jump headfirst into action plans and to-do lists so quickly that they don't spend any time upfront thinking about how their idea can be made even better just through some simple tweaks, then watching how people respond and changing strategy to keep up with the feedback.

Killer ideas aren't just born that way; they are refined and adapted, sometimes over years and decades, until they are just right. Each piece of feedback helps the idea become better.

In 2007, Melanie Perkins was a university student in Perth who spent some of her spare time tutoring her classmates in how to use graphic-design computer programs. Software like Adobe's Photoshop and Lightroom were expensive, clunky and complicated. 'It would take a whole semester just for people to learn where the buttons were, let alone how to design something that actually looked good,' Melanie has said.[78]

It wasn't just knowing which buttons to click; Melanie and her boyfriend, Cliff Obrecht, could see that the entire process surrounding design, from purchasing software to learning it, buying stock photos and templates, creating the designs, making revisions and then sending the final designs to someone, was fragmented and expensive.

They sensed an opportunity, and thought they'd test it out by starting small with one segment of the market: designing school yearbooks in Australia. 'It seemed like there was a huge need,' Melanie said.[79] 'My mum is a teacher and had always been responsible for the yearbook at her school, which took her hundreds of hours... the huge need for a better solution was obvious.'

They took over the living room of Melanie's mum as their first office and began finding people to build their software for them, as well as ringing schools all around Australia to sell their product. They recruited their family members to help send out marketing materials, lick stamps and mail books. 'It was all very manual,' recalled Melanie, 'but we learnt the ropes and got to learn about running and growing a business, developing software and marketing. Importantly, we learned the fundamentals of how to create a product that provides enough value that people are happy to pay for it.'

They could also see a rising tide in front of them. 'In days gone by... communication was predominantly words-based,' Melanie explained. 'Newspapers were words-based, sales pitches were words-based. Everything was essentially very much word-based.' The rise of social media and 'digital everything' meant that visual communication was becoming the status quo, and it was important that everyone, just not graphic designers, had the ability to design.

It took Melanie and Cliff a few more years to bring others on board with their vision, eventually convincing a technical co-founder, Cameron Adams, to join them. By this time, they'd already received dozens of rejections from their initial pitches: 'My biggest issue is physical distance,' wrote an investor from the US. 'I'm honestly, and unfortunately, not comfortable doing a deal in Australia.' Some questioned the valuation of the company, while others still just couldn't see the vision. Melanie listened to feedback whenever she presented, and used those questions to refine the pitch, and eventually the product itself.

When a potential investor in one meeting queried the size of the opportunity, Melanie added a new slide showing the size of each of the markets they could disrupt: the stock photo industry (then worth US$1.8 billion), design services (US$24 billion), desktop publishing (US$32.6 billion) and the print industry (US$80 billion).

When another investor asked if there was actually a gap in the market, the co-founders mapped out who their competition was on two axes, showing there was an opportunity for a company to own the quadrant of 'low-budget' and 'complete creative freedom'. Every pitch was an opportunity to refine the company's sense of purpose, and to make it easier to understand.

One of their early investors was Wesley Chan, the founder of Google Analytics. The typical pitch he saw was over 100 slides of information, whereas Melanie's final pitch was only 23 slides. 'I've seen a lot of founders coming in to do pitches... feel that, in order to get their point across, they have to throw everything at the person they're pitching to,' he has said. 'It's the exact opposite that actually makes a great pitch: "How do I prioritise the most important thing for me to get across?"'

The first round of investment for their company, Canva, valued the new business at US$8 million, and finally gave them enough funds to spend a year building the product before officially launching in 2013. Not only did Melanie and Cliff use feedback to make their pitches better before they even had a product, they employed user feedback every step of the way to refine their product to make it simple for people to use for the first time.

Their user testing told them that it wasn't just the buttons and tools that stopped customers from creating great designs in other software like Photoshop; it was people's own belief that they couldn't design. 'In order for Canva to take off, we needed to change their own self-belief about their design abilities... we needed to make them feel happy and confident clicking around,' Melanie pointed out. The growing team spent months perfecting the onboarding experience, using gamification to encourage play and paying attention to how people felt at every stage of the process through regular user testing: they wanted to see if users felt scared to click around and dejected by their own bad designs, or happy and confident once they had explored the site and discovered their own completed designs looked pretty good.

Canva found an audience right from launch, and in less than a year 330,000 people had used Canva to create one million designs.[80] The rest is Australian startup history, with Canva growing so much every year that by 2021 it was valued at US$40 billion, the most valuable privately held software company in the world, with 2,200 staff and more than 60 million monthly users. Not bad for a business that's been around for less than a decade.

Once your idea is out in the world and people are using it and giving feedback, knowing who to listen to, how to be receptive and which parts of your idea to adapt are key to making your idea a killer one. There's a difference between listening, and *really* listening. Active listening is when you make a conscious effort to not just hear the words someone is saying, but also what is not being said verbally. People give feedback in lots of ways: some might write a review, others vote with their wallets, but sometimes it's the *actions* of consumers you need to observe and learn from to see where the problems, or opportunities, lie.

You can apply this same concept to any creative project. On 7 May 1998, the 23rd and final episode of the fourth season of *Friends* aired. The series was already a massive worldwide hit, and the episode (spoiler alert!) featured Monica, Joey, Chandler and Ross and eventually Rachel heading to London for Ross's wedding. Aside from the usual wedding dramas, there was a secondary storyline in which Monica and Chandler hooked up and had a brief holiday romance. At least, it was meant to be a brief one. During a panel to promote her new show *Grace and Frankie*, *Friends* co-creator Marta Kauffman revealed that the relationship between Monica and Chandler was intended to be just a one-night stand. 'We had no idea what response that was going to get,' she said.[81] 'We thought it was going to be funny and we were going to get rid of it.'

But the audience wasn't having it. The screams and cheering during the live taping of the scene where they got together were so loud and continuous that they surprised everyone working on the show. 'Suddenly, the audience told us they had been waiting for that… we had to rethink how we were going to keep going and change the relationship.' They quickly modified the script for the next season, and Monica and Chandler's romantic relationship ended up becoming the longest on the show, continuing for the next six seasons. Co-creator David Crane said they used the same method of listening to live audience feedback to make the show funnier. 'We would listen to the audience and if a joke didn't land, even if we loved that joke, they were telling us it's not good enough,' he said during a reunion special.[82] 'So we would put our heads together and try to beat it.'

Listening to how people interact with your idea, then adapting your strategy to suit it, is one of the hallmarks of an idea that gets better with time. It's also a sign that you are thinking holistically about the entire process of creative thinking and how every step interacts with the others.

Joanna Keeling, the director of advisory consultancy Ibis Ideas, has conducted research with over 100 companies all over the world to determine why some of them are better than others at the entire process, from ideas generation to ongoing tweaks. Ibis Ideas identified five common behaviours of organisations – called Ideas-Led Organisations, or ILOs – that successfully put ideas at their core and were able to think their way through most obstacles, changes or hardships.[83]

- They value new ideas, and demand them by making them everyone's responsibility.
- They generate new ideas, and understand the intellectual curiosity, space and diversity of talent and experience required to bring them to life.
- They know how to curate ideas, then develop and clearly communicate their own mechanisms for doing so.
- They nurture ideas, and do not let red tape or internal politics inadvertently kill them in infancy.
- They activate ideas, and place a heavy premium on the outcomes that they achieve.

They discovered that Ideas-Led Organisations didn't just concentrate on one of these areas at a time, but had systems in place that allowed ideas to be at different stages of development and activation at any given time. That way, it takes the form of a loop that develops and maintains its own momentum, keeping fresh ideas created and brought to life. That's how you integrate the learnings from feedback to make an idea better.

However, getting to that stage takes a lot of time and effort. 'We met very few organisations who felt they were doing all five really well,' says Joanna. 'There are some organisations that are amazing at generating new ideas, but didn't nurture them enough until they become real. There are other organisations that are so good at activating ideas – and once they go they are amazing – but there are very few individuals who are good at all of that at once. You really need lots of different types of people with different skillsets.'

One of the most surprising results from their research was which company ticked almost every box in becoming an Ideas-Led Organisation. Was it one of the sexy movie studios or fancy design agencies? Not at all, explains Joanna. 'They were a plumbing equipment manufacturer – couldn't be less sexy – but they do a lot of the stages really well. They source ideas from everywhere, not just their people but from outside... It's a place where it's completely safe to have a bad idea and to move on. There is absolutely no blame going on, you're expected to contribute... It's very much a shared sense of responsibility,' she stops before adding: 'But it wasn't very glamorous!'

Navigate by Your North Star

Once your idea is out in the world, you will get a chance to see how people interact with it, and people will volunteer feedback. *I don't like this. You should change that. Why don't you do that?* Not all feedback is equal, so it's important to know who you should respond to, and what you can ignore.

It helps to be super clear on why you're doing something, or to identify your 'North Star', to help decide who to listen to. A North Star is your clear articulation of where your creative idea is heading. Writer, host and journalist Marc Fennell does this for every project he's involved in. It's a technique he picked up from podcasting expert Eric Nuzum, author of the book *Make Noise*. 'A North Star is not a motto, or a public-facing statement,' explains Marc, 'but it is the engine of your product. The reason you have it is because when you have all avenues open to you and you can take a story literally anywhere, you want to be able to triangulate everything against a singular idea.'

A North Star is basically another name for 'the idea in a sentence'. If you've completed the IRL exercise in Step 7 to summarise your idea in a page, a paragraph and a sentence, then you can use the same single sentence to help guide and keep you on track.

Take, for example, the podcast series *It Burns*, which Marc created for Audible. The series looked into the scandal-plagued race to breed the world's hottest chilli. It was released in 2019 and named one of the best podcasts of the year by The Webby Awards, *The Times*, Gizmodo and *Esquire*. A lot of Marc's ideas come from conversations. A random chat about hot chillies with a colleague led him down a rabbit-hole of research until he realised there were a lot of questions he couldn't find the answers to, which became the basis for the series.

As he recorded gigabytes of audio interviews and met dozens of people, he realised he was getting a bit stuck in all of the information. That's where his 'North Star', or idea in a sentence, came in handy. Marc wrote down a single line to summarise what the series was about that was just for him:

The idea for *It Burns* in a sentence: *The race to breed the world's hottest chilli unveils a world of immense pain.*

'Everybody in that story,' says Marc, 'was using physical pain to deal with their emotional pain, because they all had a bunch of personal problems.' That was the through-line he kept returning to every time he hit a brick wall in the process of making the series. 'No public person needs to know that engine. In fact, in some ways it's better if they never know it, and it's just revealed through the characters in the story.'

Marc's second series for Audible was *Nut Jobs*, an investigation that looked into the world of nuts. Yes, nuts. The guiding light for that production was as follows.

The idea for *Nut Jobs* in a sentence: *A $10 million heist of nuts unveils just how insecure our food supply really is.*

Nut Jobs was a critical success, receiving over 7,000 reviews on Audible that Marc pored over to find insights to make future series even better. 'I learned a lot about where people's attention waned, where they felt the story was pulling too long a bow, and what parts of the pay-off at the end they really loved,' he says. 'It directly shaped how we tackled the mysteries in my next series.'

That next show was *Stuff the British Stole*, a podcast for the Australian Broadcasting Corporation focusing on the murky reign of the British Empire and the questionable objects collected during the process of colonisation that are currently displayed in museums all over the world. Again Marc summarised the series into a North Star to keep him on track when the amount of audio recordings, scribbled notes and half-written scripts got overwhelming.

The idea for *Stuff the British Stole* in a sentence: *Investigating objects stolen by the British Empire reveals the complex impact of colonialism.*

Wherever possible, Marc tries to explain his ideas to other people face-to-face. This allows him to pick up on subtle social clues and reactions, an important part of really 'hearing' someone's feedback on an idea. 'Often people won't tell you that they don't think something is a good idea,' says Marc, 'but their body language can't lie.' When you explain an idea to someone, you should watch their face and emotions as they react to it. 'You can see when their eyes glaze over,' says Marc, 'or when they're uncomfortable or confused.' You can use those cues to refine your idea, and the pitch, until they're easily understood.

Listen to Your Audience

Anthony and Alex Zaccaria are two brothers from Melbourne who started a digital agency with their friend Nick Humphreys. The agency ran social media campaigns, created content and put on events for lots of music festivals, artists and culture brands. It was a good business, with a few dozen staff and some of the leading record labels and musicians in the country as clients, but it was also hard work. A lot of the work had to be done manually, involving teams of people sitting at their desks, constantly updating Facebook ad accounts with new details to keep on top of their clients' needs. Their agency also ran social media accounts on platforms like Instagram for their clients, and they found that every time they wanted to promote something new, they would have to go back to edit the bio on their clients' Instagram pages, and could only ever promote one thing at a time. 'Your music lives on one platform, your ticketing on another, your merch on another,' says Anthony. 'It was really fragmented as to how you do them all together. That's quite true across a lot of areas, but very apparent in music.'

They saw an easy solution in a single URL that could link off to multiple places at once, and their developer built the first iteration of their product, Linktree, in six hours. They tested it out with their own clients first, and then allowed other people to create their own page of links. The feedback from early users was very positive. 'Their main reaction was "Why have I never thought of this?"', says Anthony. 'From there people were like, "Oh holy shit, this is so useful. I never realised I needed this until I actually had it."'

Linktree's user base steadily grew as the word spread of this elegant solution. Six months in, Grammy Award-winning singer Alicia Keys signed up to Linktree, and the ensuing publicity saw 3,000 people sign up in one day. 'That was obviously a huge moment of validation for us,' says Anthony. 'It wasn't just small business people who were in our sphere that were using it. It showed us that an artists like Alicia Keys, with all the resources of a major label and a big management team, has the same problem as all of us.'

These early users gave them lots of feedback: some wanted to be able to update their links instantly, while others wanted to be able to link directly to social commerce sites to sell things seamlessly. Their second moment of validation came when they launched a paid version, with more ability to customise and view analytics. 'That was really cool to see,' says Anthony. 'We thought, "People are actually paying for this thing. I think we're onto something here. It could be a profitable business."'

Linktree is a great example of killer thinking that seems so obvious in retrospect: a single link to house all of your important links on the internet in one place. It was originally created to solve a need that Alex, Anthony and Nick had and is now used by over 18 million people, with more than 30,000 new sign-ups every single day. The three founders have now raised US$55.7 million in funding to help expand their global reach, social commerce tools and maintain their market-leading position.[84] They listen intently to their customers to refine their product, from regular surveys, support chat and a dedicated user success team who manage some of their most important clients and collate their feedback into new features. They also trawl through gigabytes of data on what people are clicking on and how they actually use the site. Anthony says it's important to balance what people say they want with the vision the founders have for the business. 'If you just do everything users said, you'd be chasing your tail all the time trying to please everybody,' he says. 'And you'd end up with a product that looks like Myspace twenty years ago!'

Linktree would not exist as an idea if they hadn't been actively listening to the problems that their clients faced, and then adapting the product based on feedback as the audience grew alongside it. Listening with open ears means being guided by the users of the product in the right direction, and continuing to refine the product to make it better. When used the right way, and acted on at the right time, feedback can be the boost you need to turn your idea from good to killer.

IRL

Step 8: Listen with Open Ears

Learn to be an active listener who can identify and act on feedback. Some businesses and people are more adept at it than others, and it's useful to know how open you are to new ideas.

Exercise 14: Creativity Scale

How much do you value ideas? It doesn't matter if you work for a company, lead one yourself or are a solo thinker, you can take this test based on Ibis Ideas' work with Ideas-Led Organisations to determine how well you score on the entire creative process.

1. Rate your business, or yourself personally, in these areas.
Each of the five questions looks at the skills needed to nurture, protect and execute great ideas. If you're doing this test for yourself, just replace 'your company' with 'you'.

Give yourself a rating from 0 to 5 on each scale when you answer each question.

1. How much does your company value new ideas?

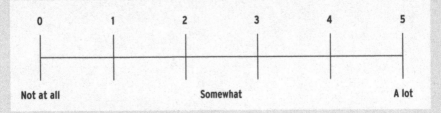

2. How well does your company generate new ideas?

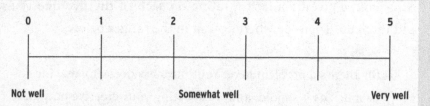

3. How well does your company know how to curate new ideas?

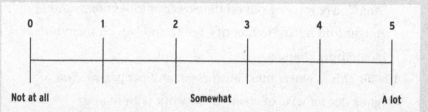

4. How well does your company nurture ideas?

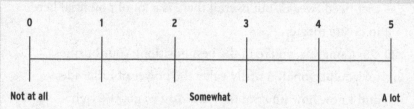

5. How well does your company activate ideas?

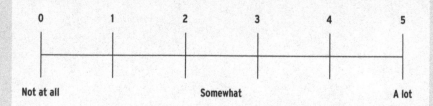

2. Add up your scores.

After you've given yourself a rating on each of the five questions, add them up. Then see where you sit in the ranges below.

0–10: There's a problem here. Your business doesn't value ideas as much as it should, and it's affecting your creative output. You need to shift the culture by concentrating on each of the five areas and identifying what or who the main blockers are. You're missing out on the power of killer ideas, and might find it hard to identify, refine and launch them unless something changes.

10–20: This is where most businesses, and people, sit. You've got a decent level of creativity to work with in your organisation, and with some help can make it even better. There are most likely areas you're going great in, and others that need tweaks, but overall there is a lot of potential here to create magic.

20–25: Congrats, you're in the best position! Your business (or you personally) really value the power of killer ideas and know how integral they are. You've got the right environment around you to cultivate lots of killer ideas and bring them to life. So what are you waiting for?

Fast Takeaways

1. Killer ideas aren't born that way: they are refined and adapted, sometimes over years and decades, until they are just right.
2. Every piece of feedback can help an idea become better.
3. Knowing who to listen to, how to be receptive and which parts of your idea to adapt are the keys to making your idea truly great.
4. Organisations that are great at creativity have some common behaviours: they value and generate new ideas, and know how to curate, nurture and activate ideas.
5. You don't need to just listen to feedback; you need to properly hear it.

Summary

So, that was a book about ideas.

Not just any old ideas, however: it was about the ideas that have the potential to disrupt industries, save lives, move markets and change minds. If that feels too daunting, please don't worry. Every killer idea started off as the germ of a thought inside someone's head before it became exceptional, and you can use the same thinking and processes to solve almost any problem you want.

Killer ideas don't come along every day – they are special ideas that benefit lots of people and are kind, impactful, loved, lasting, easy and repeatable. When they do arise, you now have some of the tools available to recognise them, massage them into shape and launch them into the world. You can use this mythology that we've built systematically from the ground up to help you think more creatively and solve problems in every aspect of your work and life. All you need to do is remember to follow the Eight Steps that make up the key to killer thinking (starting from the bottom):

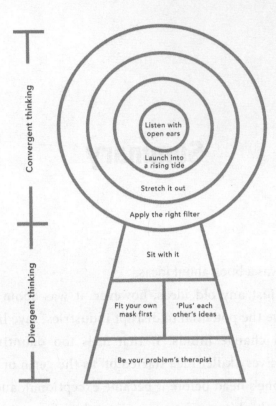

The first four steps involve divergent thinking, where we come up with as many ideas as we can, and the final four steps are where we use convergent thinking to home in on and perfect the best ones.

Step 1: Be Your Problem's Therapist
Take the time at the beginning of a project to absorb as much information as you can, and try to understand every single aspect of your problem better than anyone else.

Step 2: Fit Your Own Mask First
Group creative sessions are useful, but they are a thousand times more effective if you do individual ideation first. You need to put on your own mask before you can properly help others fit theirs.

Step 3: 'Plus' Each Other's Ideas

Coming up with ideas with other people should be fun! Your Cerebration sessions can help you generate lots of ideas that build on top of everyone's ideas.

Step 4: Sit with It

If you don't let creativity work its magic, you're not going to get to the most creative solutions to your problems. So give your ideas some space, inputs and time to develop properly.

Step 5: Apply the Right Filter

Once you've got some good ideas, you then need a clear, customised filter that helps you narrow them down to just the ones with the best potential.

Step 6: Stretch It Out

Good ideas can be stretched by focusing on who benefits from them. The more people who 'win', the better the idea.

Step 7: Launch into a Rising Tide

The timing of when you launch an idea is almost as important as the idea itself. Think carefully about when is the right time to share your idea with the world.

Step 8: Listen with Open Ears

Knowing how to actively listen to your audience, and then incorporating their feedback into your product or service, are key to making your idea a killer one that has potential for a deep impact.

And that's it! They are the Eight Steps to killer thinking that anyone can follow. You've got brilliant ideas inside you, and armed with these tools you'll now be able to recognise, filter, refine and expand them into ones with big potential. I seriously love hearing from you about your creative ideas and how you're bringing them to life, so please head to timduggan.com.au to reach out and say hello.

Once you've mastered these Eight Steps you can apply them to everything in your life and work. Everything begins with an idea, and now it's over to you to come up with some of your own.

Endnotes

1   Poppenk, Jordan and Tseng, Julie, 'Brain meta-state transitions demarcate thoughts across task contexts exposing the mental noise of trait neuroticism, *Nature Communications*, July 2020, https://neurosciencenews.com/thought-worms-16639/

2   Zaki, Jamil, 'Kindness Contagion', 26 July 2016, *Scientific American*, USA, https://www.scientificamerican.com/article/kindness-contagion/

3   Brown, Brené, *Dare To Lead: Brave Work. Tough Conversations. Whole Hearts.*, 2018, Vermilion, USA

4   Gill-Sommerhauser, Collin, 'SAP Speaker Series presents Google's Chief Innovation Evangelist Dr. Frederick G. Pferdt', 5 February 2020, HanaHaus, USA, https://www.hanahaus.com/blog-1/frederik-g-pferdt

5   Balinbin, Arjay L., 'Empathy is the skill of the future, Google says', 14 February 2021, *Business World*, USA, https://www.bworldonline.com/empathy-is-the-skill-of-the-future-google-says/

6   De Graft, Brian, 'Meet Luis von Ahn, the man you've worked for, without knowing it', 17 August 2016, *The Next Web*, USA https://thenextweb.com/news/meet-luis-van-ahn-man-youve-worked-without-knowing

7   Appiah, Lidz-Ama, 'Slave-free chocolate: a not-so guilty pleasure', 7 June 2017, *CNN*, USA, https://edition.cnn.com/2017/06/02/world/tonys-chocolonely-slavery-free-chocolate/index.html

8   Thomsen, Simon, 'Melbourne waste startup raises $5 million, 18 November 2021, *Startup Daily*, Australia, https://www.startupdaily.net/2021/11/melbourne-waste-startup-bardee-raises-5-million-seed-round/

9   Our Impact, OzHarvest, https://www.ozharvest.org/

10   Hirsch, Lily E., *Music In American Crime Prevention and Punishment*, 15 November 2015, University of Michigan Press, USA

11   McFadyen, William, 'Manilow a secret weapon', 13 August 2016, *The Sydney Morning Herald*, Australia, https://www.theage.com.au/national/manilow-a-secret-weapon-20060813-ge2wuu.html

12   Lagan, Bernard, 'Q: How do you get rid of a gang of boy racers? A: Play Barry Manilow at full volume', 18 July 2006, *The Times*, UK, https://www.thetimes.co.uk/article/q-how-do-you-get-rid-of-a-gang-of-boy-racers-a-play-barry-manilow-at-full-volume-nf7dfpfxnt9

13   Goodby, Jeff and Silverstein, Rich, 'Jeff Goodby and Rich Silverstein teach Advertising and Creativity', 2020, *Masterclass*, USA, https://www.masterclass.com/classes/jeff-goodby-and-rich-silverstein-teach-advertising-and-creativity

14   Sternberg, Robert J., 'The Nature of Creativity', *Creativity Research Journal*, 2006, Vol. 18, No. 1, Tufts University, USA

15   MacLoed, Hugh, *Ignore Everybody: and 39 other keys to creativity*, 2009, Portfolio, USA

16   Ritter, Simone M. & Mostert, Nel M., 'Enhancement of Creative Thinking Skills Using a Cognitive-Based Creativity Training', *Journal of Cognitive Enhancement*, 2017, https://doi.org/10.1007/s41465-016-0002-3

17   Runco, Mark A., 'Creativity', *Annual Review of Psychology*, 2004, https://www.annualreviews.org/doi/full/10.1146/annurev.psych.55.090902.141502

18   Gilbert, Elizabeth, 'Liz's free 10-step writing school', 31 August 2019, Instagram, https://www.instagram.com/p/B11D_wWBY_g/?igshid=1q4edpzq69gpg

19   Schneider, Benjamin, 'The evolution of airline safety videos', 23 December 2017, *Bloomberg*, USA, https://www.bloomberg.com/news/articles/2017-12-22/the-evolution-of-airline-safety-videos

20   Sheeran, Ed, 'Let songwriting flow', 2014, Recording Academy Grammy Awards, USA, https://www.grammy.com/professional-development/video/ed-sheeran-2014-let-songwriting-flow

21   Pilkington, Ed, 'Jonathan Franzen: "I must be nearing the end of my career – people are strating to approve."', 25 September 2010, *The Guardian*, UK, https://www.theguardian.com/books/2010/sep/25/jonathan-franzen-interview

22   Austin, Tom, 'AND1's Three Hundred "No's"', 9 August 2017, Medium, USA, https://medium.com/@Tomyani/near-death-and-1s-300-no-s-ad4da029b1d5

23   Wolf, Gary, 'Steve Jobs: The Next Insanely Great Thing', 1 February 1996, *Wired*, USA https://www.wired.com/1996/02/jobs-2/

24   Heath, Alex, 'Steve Jobs wanted to make an iCar', 17 May 2012, *Cult of Mac*, USA, https://www.cultofmac.com/167806/steve-jobs-wanted-to-design-an-icar-before-he-died/

25   Ferriss, Tim, 'Marc Randolph on building Netflix, battling Blockbuster, negotiating with Amazon/Jeff Bezos, and scraping the barnacles off the

hull', 1 February 2021, The Tim Ferris Show podcast, USA, https://tim.
blog/2021/02/01/marc-randolph-transcript/

26   Bradley, Laura, 'Netflix nabs Seinfeld streaming rights in $500 million-plus
deal', 16 September 2019, *Vanity Fair*, USA, https://www.vanityfair.com/
hollywood/2019/09/seinfeld-netflix-streaming-deal

27   Ferriss, Tim, 'Jerry Seinfeld – a comedy legend's systems, routines and methods
for success', 9 December 2020, The Tim Ferris Show podcast, USA, https://tim.
blog/2020/12/09/jerry-seinfeld-transcript/

28   The World's 50 Best Restaurants, The List, USA, https://www.theworlds50best.
com/the-list/31-40/Alinea.html

29   Michelin Guide United States, Alinea, https://guide.michelin.com/en/illinois/
chicago/restaurant/alinea

30   Foodie by Glam, 'Allen & Alinea: One man's odyssey through an iconic
cookbook', 12 November 2014, YouTube, https://www.youtube.com/
watch?v=SLPUGIftRq4

31   The Alinea Project, Kickstarter, https://www.kickstarter.com/
projects/1050038100/the-alinea-project

32   Van Zandt, Emily, 'Review: The Aviary', 4 May 2011, *Chicago Tribune*, USA,
https://www.chicagotribune.com/redeye/redeye-review-the-aviary-20120123-
story.html

33   The Alinea Group, The Aviary Cocktail Book, Kickstarter, https://www.
kickstarter.com/projects/thealineagroup/the-aviary-cocktail-book/description

34   Hemberger, Allen, The Alinea Project, Chicago Ideas, https://www.
chicagoideas.com/videos/the-alinea-project

35   Dobbins, Amanda, 'Fact-Checking the Age-Old Rumors of Walt Disney's Dark
Side', 11 December 2013, *Vulture*, USA, https://www.vulture.com/2013/12/walt-
disney-anti-semitism-racism-sexism-frozen-head.html

36   'In Walt's Own Words: Plussing Disneyland', 17 July 2014, The Walt Disney
Family Museum, https://www.waltdisney.org/blog/walts-own-words-plussing-
disneyland

37   Thomas, Bob, *Disney's Art of Animation: From Mickey Mouse to Hercules*, 1997,
Hyperion, New York

38   Osborn, Alex, *How To 'Think Up'*, McGraw Hill, 1942, USA

39   Asimov, Isaac, 'Isaac Asimov asks 'how do people get new ideas?', 20 October
2014, *MIT Technology Review*, USA, https://www.technologyreview.
com/2014/10/20/169899/isaac-asimov-asks-how-do-people-get-new-ideas/

40   Duhigg, Charles, 'What Google learned from its quest to build the ultimate
team', 25 February 2016, *The New York Times*, USA, https://www.nytimes.
com/2016/02/28/magazine/what-google-learned-from-its-quest-to-build-the-
perfect-team.html

41   Catmull, Ed, 'How Pixar Fosters Collective Creativity', September 2008, *Harvard Business Review*, USA, https://hbr.org/2008/09/how-pixar-fosters-collective-creativity

42   Hansche, Melanie, 26 March 2019, 'This Aussie Fish Butcher is the World's Most Creative – and Controversial – Seafood Chef', *Food&Wine*, https://www.foodandwine.com/chefs/josh-niland-australian-seafood

43   Anderson, Sam, 'The Weirdly Enduring Appeal of Weird Al Yankovic', 9 April 2020, *The New York Times*, https://www.nytimes.com/2020/04/09/magazine/weird-al-yankovic.html

44   Oppezzo, Marily and Schwart, Daniel L., 'Give Your Ideas Some Legs: The Positive Effect of Walking on Creative Thinking', 2014, *Journal of Experimental Psychology*, Stanford University, USA https://www.apa.org/pubs/journals/releases/xlm-a0036577.pdf

45   Solnit, Rebecca, *Wanderlust: A History of Walking*, 2000, Penguin, USA

46   Prip-Buus, Mogens, 'Jorn Utzon's Sydney Opera House', 2018, Drawing Matter, Australia, https://drawingmatter.org/mogens-prip-buus-jorn-utzons-sydney-opera-house/

47   Fink, A., Koschutnig, K., Benedek, M., Reishofer, G., Ischebeck, A., Weiss, E.M., Ebner, F., 'Stimulating creativity via the exposure to other people's ideas', 2012, Division of Biological Psychology, Institute of Psychology, University of Graz, Austria

48   King, Stephen, *On Writing: A Memoir of the Craft*, 2010, Hodder and Stoughton, USA

49   Sio, U. N., Monaghan, P., & Ormerod, T., 'Sleep on it, but only if it is difficult: effects of sleep on problem solving', *Memory & cognition*, 2013, https://doi.org/10.3758/s13421-012-0256-7

50   Tusa, John, 'Anish Kapoor, In Conversation with John Tusa', AnishKapoor.com, https://anishkapoor.com/180/in-conversation-with-john-tusa-2

51   Killingsworth, Matthew, and Gilbert, Daniel, 'A Wandering Mind is an Unhappy Mind', 12 November 2010, Science, USA, https://www.science.org/doi/10.1126/science.1192439

52   Lehrer, Jonah, 'The Virtues of Daydreaming', 5 June 2012, *The New Yorker*, USA, https://www.newyorker.com/tech/frontal-cortex/the-virtues-of-daydreaming

53   Heath, Dan, and Heath, Chip, *Switch: How to change things when change is hard*, 2010, Penguin Random House, USA

54   Wood, Deborah, 'Decreasing Disruptions Reduces Medical Errors', 2009, *RN.com*, USA, https://www.rn.com/Pages/ResourceDetails.aspx?id=3369

55   Eyal, Nir, *Indistractable: How to Control Your Attention and Choose Your Life*, 2019, BenBella Books, USA

56   Ferriss, Tim, 'Jerry Seinfeld – a comedy legend's systems, routines and methods for success', 9 December 2020, The Tim Ferris Show podcast, USA, https://tim. blog/2020/12/09/jerry-seinfeld-transcript/

57   ibid. Ferriss, Tim, 'Jerry Seinfeld – a comedy legend's systems, routines and methods for success.'

58   Swan, David, 'Find Your Culture: Netflix Founder', 20 August 2021, *The Australian*, Australia, https://www.theaustralian.com.au/business/ technology/find-your-culture-netflix-cofounder-marc-randolph/news- story/1b2e695867d21d28ba0d5b7cee918525

59   Buckmaster, Luke, 'Why is "You Can't Ask That" one of the most successful shows on the ABC', 11 July 2018, *The Guardian*, Australia, https://www. theguardian.com/tv-and-radio/2018/jul/11/why-is-you-cant-ask-that-one-of- the-most-successful-shows-on-the-abc

60   Mediaweek, 'Annual survey lists ABC's You Can't Ask That amongst world's hottest TV formats', 17 May 2021, https://www.mediaweek.com.au/annual- survey-lists-abcs-you-cant-ask-that-amongst-worlds-hottest-tv-formats/

61   Daffey, Mark, 'Silo art trails breathing new life into regional towns', 3 March 2021, *Explore*, Australia, https://www.exploretravel.com.au/experience/silo-art- trails-breathing-new-life-into-regional-towns/

62   Darling, Alexander, 'Silo art attracts visitors but more needed to keep tourist dollars, study finds', 26 August 2021, *ABC News*, Australia, https://www. abc.net.au/news/2021-08-26/australian-silo-art-study-investment-regional- tourism-impact/100409170

63   Kuefler, Kayla, 'Love at First Swipe: The Evolution of Online Dating', *Stylight*, USA, https://www.stylight.com.au/Magazine/Lifestyle/Love-First-Swipe- Evolution-Online-Dating/

64   Ortega, Josue and Hergovich, Phillip, 'The Strength of Absent Ties: Social Integration via Online Dating', 2017, *Physics and Society*, Cornell University, USA, https://arxiv.org/abs/1709.10478

65   Hartmans, Avery, and Akhtar, Allana, 'How Tinder and Hinge Owner Match Group Grew to Dominate the Country's Online Dating Market – But Let Bumble Get Away', 4 February 2021, *Business Insider*, Australia, https:// www.businessinsider.com.au/what-is-match-group-history-of-tinder-parent- company-2021-1

66   Carman, Ashley, 'Tinder made $1.2 billion last year off people who can't stop swiping', 4 February 2020, *The Verge*, USA, https://www.theverge. com/2020/2/4/21123057/tinder-1-billion-dollars-match-group-revenue- earnings

67   Bilton, Nick, 'Tinder, the fast growing dating app, taps an age-old truth', 29 October 2014, *The New York Times*, USA, https://www.nytimes.com/

2014/10/30/fashion/tinder-the-fast-growing-dating-app-taps-an-age-old-truth.
html

68   Soffer, Rebecca, 'These 3 Innovators are the Next Big Thing In Business', 15
December 2015, *Marie Claire*, USA, https://www.marieclaire.com/culture/
a17342/next-big-thing-vision-quest/

69   Palmer-Derrien, Stephanie, 'Bumble's IPO Makes Whitney Wolfe Herd a
Billionaire, and Youngest Woman to Take a Tech Unicorn Public', 12 February
2021, *Women's Agenda*, Australia, https://womensagenda.com.au/business/
bumbles-ipo-makes-whitney-wolfe-herd-a-billionaire-and-youngest-woman-
to-take-a-tech-unicorn-public/

70   Gluyas, Alex, 'Climate change "biggest investment opportunity since the
internet"', 1 September 2021, *Australian Financial Review*, Australia, https://
www.afr.com/wealth/personal-finance/climate-change-biggest-investment-
opportunity-since-the-internet-20210826-p58m4w

71   Five Fifty: The Quickening, McKinsey Quarterly, McKinsey & Company,
USA, https://www.mckinsey.com/business-functions/strategy-and-corporate-
finance/our-insights/five-fifty-the-quickening

72   Spangler, Todd, '"The Queen's Gambit" Scores as Netflix Most-Watched
Scripted Limited Series To Date", 23 November 2020, *Variety*, USA,
https://variety.com/2020/digital/news/queens-gambit-netflix-viewing-
record-1234838090/

73   Ogilvy, David, *Ogilvy on Advertising*, 1985, Vintage Books, USA

74   Carmichael, Evan, 'You're a Big Fish in a Puddle....so What?', 5 April 2016,
YouTube, USA, https://www.youtube.com/watch?v=8pALdP35zAU

75   Dowling, Stephen, 'The cheap pen that changed writing forever', 30 October
2020, *BBC*, UK, https://www.bbc.com/future/article/20201028-history-of-the-
ballpoint-pen

76   Phaidon Editors, 'Everyday Icon #3 The BIC Biro', *The Design Book*, Phaidon,
USA, https://www.phaidon.com/agenda/design/articles/2011/october/19/
everyday-icon-3-the-bic-biro

77   Smith, David, 'It's 70 today, but our favourite pen just keeps rolling
along', 15 June 2008, *The Guardian*, UK, https://www.theguardian.com/
technology/2008/jun/15/news#

78   Canva Create Conference 2021: Day 01 Sessions, Canva, YouTube https://www.
youtube.com/watch?v=F9kneWEgTKo

79   Perkins, Melanie, '21 Questions from Aussie Startups: Highs, Lows and Lessons
Learned During Canva's Journey So Far (Part 1)', 15 January 2018, Medium,
https://medium.com/canva/21-questions-from-aussie-startups-highs-lows-
lessons-learned-during-canvas-journey-so-far-da07723ff545

80   Lyons, Dan, 'Marketing Legend Guy Kawasaki Joins Australians Startup', 16 April 2014, Hubspot, USA, https://blog.hubspot.com/opinion/marketing-legend-guy-kawasaki-joins-canva-a-tiny-australian-startup

81   AAP, 'Monica and Chandler weren't meant to wed', 9 June 2015, *NZ Herald*, New Zealand, https://www.nzherald.co.nz/entertainment/monica-and-chandler-werent-meant-to-wed/WOR6PJSWIDQGEEUEY6JHIWEEYU/

82   Corinthios, Aurelie, 'Matthew Perry would "freak out" if Friends audience didn't laugh: "I felt like that every night"', 28 May 2021, *Yahoo Finance*, https://finance.yahoo.com/news/matthew-perry-freak-friends-audience-140000172.html

83   Ideas-Led Organisations, Ibis Ideas, UK, https://ibisideas.com/ILOs

84   Shu, Catherine, '"Link-in-bio" company Linktree raises $45M Series B for its social commerce features', 26 March 2021, Techcrunch, USA, https://techcrunch.com/2021/03/26/link-in-bio-company-linktree-raises-45m-series-b-for-its-social-commerce-features/

Acknowledgements

It takes a village to publish a book, and there was a real team effort to get this book into your hands.

Firstly, and most importantly, I want to thank every single person who read and shared my first book, *Cult Status*. You took a chance on a new author, and your feedback and encouragement genuinely fuelled me to bring this second book to life, from readers who answered my public request for suggestions for brilliant ideas to everyone who shared their favourite research on creativity. I also appreciated introductions from people like Andrew Davies who connected me to their networks. Thank you so much.

I am forever indebted to the amazing team at my publisher, Pantera Press. Lex Hirst and Tom Langshaw in Editorial are superstars in every sense of the word. Kajal Narayan in Marketing brings joy and skill to every meeting, Léa Antigny and Taliesyn Gottlieb wrangle publicity effortlessly, Kate O'Donnell copyedits with love and sensitivity, and Alison Green leads her team of 'Book Avengers' fearlessly. I always tell people how much I love being part of Pantera Press, and I mean every word.

My family are always my biggest supporters: my beautiful parents, Anna and Phil, and siblings Andrew, Chris, Rachael and their families. My mum and dad instilled a deep sense of creativity into us all from a young age, and I can trace my passion for writing and communicating straight back to them. My older brother Chris swears he's still the largest bulk-buyer of my books to give out as gifts for his clients and partners, which I'm inclined to believe, but I haven't seen all of the receipts to confirm that yet.

There are a bunch of people who are constant supporters in my life. Alex Sutcliffe was my researcher for the book who helped me wade through dozens of scientific research papers to find the relevant gold. Stig Richards sent me his fave musings on creativity, and helped inspire the Cerebrations model. Neil Ackland has taught that me real creativity takes hard work, and to never settle for just 'good enough'. Vanessa Ackland designed the front cover and incorporates killer ideas into all of her work. Finally, writing this book has brought into sharp relief the importance of positive influences early in my life, and for that I particularly want to thank my high school English teacher, Magar Etmekdjian, who passed his own love for words, reasoning and logic onto me.

Thank you to everyone I interviewed in this book for sharing your wisdom, and to Sarah Wilson, Lisa Messenger and Victoria Devine for reading advance copies of the book and giving your kind words.

This book is dedicated to my husband Ben, my biggest supporter and co-conspirator in life. We've spent most of the last year or so travelling around Australia, from Mildura to Monkey Mia, Daylesford to Darwin, as I wrote the bulk of this in a campervan, hotels and Airbnbs. You give me the inspiration to keep dreaming and the space to turn it into reality, and for that I thank – and love – you. The world really is our oyster.

Cybele Malinowski

Tim Duggan is an optimist who firmly believes in the power of business to do good. He has co-founded several digital media ventures, most notably Junkee Media, one of the leading publishers for Australian millennials.

Tim's first book, *Cult Status: How to Build a Business People Adore*, was named the Best Entrepreneurship and Small Business Book at the 2021 Australian Business Book Awards.

Tim is also the chairman of the Digital Publishers Alliance, an industry body that represents over a hundred titles from leading independent digital publishers. He began his career as a music journalist for *Rolling Stone*, and sits on several boards including the Griffin Theatre Company, Australia's new writing theatre.

Tim lives with his husband, Ben, and dog, Winnie, in Sydney.

KILLER THINKING

INTERESTED IN MORE?

For more information on *Killer Thinking*, and to download free worksheets to help you complete all of the exercises, go to

www.timduggan.com.au

Learn about long-term, sustainable success with 14 practical exercises you can do today to set up for success tomorrow.

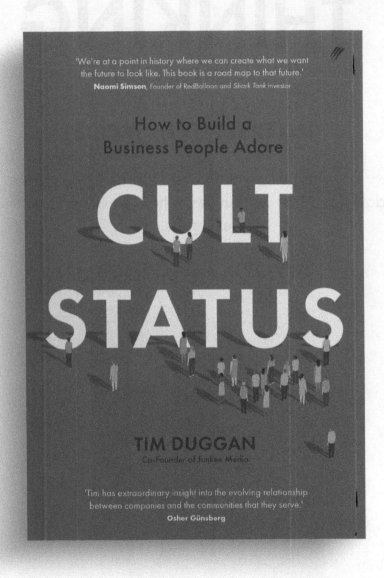

'We're at a point in history where we can create what we want the future to look like. This book is a road map to that future.'
Naomi Simson, Founder of RedBalloon and *Shark Tank* investor

How to Build a
Business People Adore

CULT
STATUS

TIM DUGGAN
Co-Founder of Junkee Media

'Tim has extraordinary insight into the evolving relationship between companies and the communities that they serve.'
Osher Günsberg

PANTERA PRESS

SPARKING
IMAGINATION,
CONVERSATION
& CHANGE

'Shows hope is not dead by a long shot.'
--- Weekly Times ---

'Glimpses of Utopia provided me the rarest thing in these grim times: hope.'
--- BENJAMIN LAW, Author of *The Inner Self* ---

'Jess Scully has scoured the world for the best ideas to fix this mess we're in.'
--- JESS HILL, *See What You Made Me Do* ---

SPARKING
IMAGINATION,
CONVERSATION
& CHANGE

'Self-made, self-motivated and infectiously self-assured,
Flex plays both forthright coach and open-hearted
student of life in this practical, empowered guide to
achieving your own version of success.'

--- *ZOË FOSTER BLAKE* ---

'A joyful, confident, razor-sharp
and exquisitely modern plan to
creating success in a way that is
meaningful to you.'
ZOË FOSTER BLAKE

THE SUCCESS EXPERIMENT

FLEXMAMI's formula for knowing
what you really want and how to get it

LILLIAN AHENKAN

BUSINESS OWNER, PODCASTER, INFLUENCER, TV PRESENTER

PANTERA
PRESS

SPARKING
IMAGINATION,
CONVERSATION
& CHANGE